Please God make my mummy nice!

Help for mums
under pressure

June 1996

Hoping that this fills you
with encouragement, and
touches you with God's
love,

Blessings,

Karen Holford

x

Please God make my mummy nice!

KAREN HOLFORD

Help for mums
under pressure

AUTUMN
HOUSE

The stories 'When you get to the end of your rope', 'Of slugs, snails and butterflies' tales' and 'Away in a manger' were first published in a Devotional for Women, *The Listening Heart*, (R&H Publishing 1993), editor Rose Otis.

The stories 'Heavenly motherhood', 'A shepherd in the storm' and 'The tale of two gravestones' were first published in a Devotional for Women, *A Gift of Love*, (R&H Publishing 1994), editor Rose Otis.

The stories 'Angel in his heart' and 'The mother on the mountain' were first published in a Devotional for Women, *A Moment of Peace*, (R&H Publishing 1995), editor Rose Otis. The author thanks Review and Herald Publishing for giving their permission to reuse the above stories.

All texts are taken from the New International Bible, unless otherwise stated.

ISBN 1-873796-59-5

Published by Autumn House
Alma Park, Grantham, Lincs, NG31 9SL

Dedication

This book is dedicated to my grandmother, Edna Barber, and my mother, Kate Welch, both of whom set before me beautiful examples of what it means to blend faith in God and motherhood. And to my children, Bethany, Nathan and Joel, for teaching me more about God every day of their lives. It is also dedicated to Bernie, my husband, who has shared in this exciting journey through parenthood, and who helped to make my motherhood a possibility!

And, finally, it is for mothers and children everywhere, and especially for you, as you fill the pages with your own thoughts, ideas, prayers and memories.

Please God make my mummy nice!

CONTENTS

First thoughts

Motherhood is the hardest job I've ever done in my life, but it's also been the most exciting adventure I've ever had! After the initial novelty of a new-born baby had faded into the overflowing laundry basket, countless broken nights, and the endless cycle of tedious housework, I needed a new perspective on my life. The twenty-four-hour-shift-work of being a mum threatened to drive a wedge between myself and God. There was barely time to think, let alone pray, and every minute of the day seemed to be filled with one pressing crisis or another. But slowly the realization dawned on me that God was all around me, in the little details of my life, if only I would learn to look and listen. Once I started to understand all the things that I could learn about God's love for me as His child, and as a mother of His children, life took on a whole new outlook. Some days I would find God in the most unexpected places. It was like a spiritual game of Hide and Seek. The greatest adventure of my life! Instead of losing touch with God, I found I was growing closer and closer to Him!

This book is filled with the stories of my discoveries, and I share them with you, not because they are unique, but because you've probably been there too, and together we can learn more about God's incredible parental love.

The stories are like little treasures, tucked away in my heart, but the book is not just my story. There's room for your stories too, with places for you to share your own experiences, hopes, laughter and tears. You can read this book on your own, use it as a work-book with a group of other mothers, or you could swop ideas and responses with another mum, who may be hungry for fellowship and friendship, just like you.

However you use this book, I hope and pray that it will encourage you. And, above all else, I pray that it will fill you with a wonderful sense of God's love for you, now and forever.

Blessings,

Karen Holford

Crayons in the Laundry

You never know what you are going to find when you have children, especially toddlers. Little ones have a knack of hiding things in the most unexpected places. I once discovered that Bethany had put a green wax crayon in our front-loading washing machine. It was a shame I didn't discover it until after it had been through a white boil wash! In fact, I never did find the crayon, but all the laundry was pale green! The washing machine has been a favourite place for all of the children to hide things. One of them used to put any unwanted food in it, like bits of apple, and peanut-butter sandwiches and raw carrot. Fortunately I discovered the sandwiches, but the carrot was done *al dente* by the time it rolled out of the machine with the nappies. And Joel enjoyed hiding little bits and pieces, like marbles, scrap paper and Lego bricks, inside our shoes or down our wellies.

Bethany was quite helpful. Even before she could talk she understood if something was lost, and would usually be able to show us where it was hidden, probably because she'd put it there. Nathan was like a squirrel that hid his nuts in the autumn, and always forgot where they were when he needed them. I had to renew one library book three times before we found it. After that I always wrote a list of the book titles as soon as we came home from the library, and tried to encourage him to return them to the same place on his shelf once they had been read. But nearly every time we take our books back to the library we have to renew at least one that we've temporarily mislaid.

One day baby Joel noticed that the postman had arrived. He must have watched with delight as all the letters tumbled through the door. After spending a few minutes looking at the envelopes, he posted them back out through the flap. It rained buckets that day, and my husband Bernie found the mail, soggy and ruined, blowing around our driveway in the evening.

Joel likes to hide things among our rubbish. Last week I found a ball, the TV remote control, Bethany's sock, and Joel's shoes all in the kitchen bin, together with the empty soup cans, plastic bags, eggshell and orange peel! Usually it makes us all laugh when we find things that Joel has posted into strange places! But I wasn't too pleased about the tooth-brushes I found down the toilet, even though the other children thought it was hilarious!

As a mum, it's hard to spend a long time with God each day. I try not to get out of bed until I have spent some time praying, reading, thinking things over, and planning my day with God. I haven't heard more than a dozen distraction-free sermons in the last eight years! It can be an advantage being married to a pastor with two churches, the bits I miss from a sermon one week, I may hear the next! I can't get to the house-fellowship groups unless it's our turn to host one. When the adults have their study groups at church I'm looking after the children's classes. For a long time I found this very frustrating. I wanted fellowship and I wanted to spend more time concentrating on God. But over the years I've come to find God, unexpectedly, in lots of little corners of my life and home. Being a mum is hard work, and the hardest job I'm sure I'll ever do, but, being with the children and caring for them has helped me to glimpse a perspective of God that isn't often talked about.

A thought here, a word from a child, a little event in

my life: day by day I find little pieces of mosaic, as an archaeologist discovers fragments in the sand. I can put these little glimpses of God together in my heart, and build up a wonderful picture of His love for me and for each one of us. Discovering God like this is an exciting way of life. I never know where I'll find another piece of the mosaic, so I keep on looking! Sometimes I find them in the laundry, or scribbled by a child on a scrap of paper. I may see Him in a touch, or a smile, or even a tear: He is all around me. There are many times I don't live up to my own high expectations, but He never leaves my side. He picks me up, dries my tears, whispers a word of comfort, gives me a hug, and sets me on my feet again, ever-forgiven and eternally-loved, and, hopefully, a little bit wiser.

Dear Father, thank You that You are all around me, as I care for Your little children. Help me to keep an eye open all the time, so I can find You in the unexpected, the wonderful, and even the trivial moments of my life. Amen.

Try finding God 'hiding' in an unexpected moment of your life. Write down where you found Him, why, and what you learned from the experience.

In what ways is God our 'Mother' as well as our Father?

Have you ever had a funny time in your home when a child hid something in a strange place? Jot down a few of your memories.

Waiting for the flutter

It was five-thirty in the morning, and I was already awake. I lay very still. Six months pregnant, I found that the slightest movement could still precipitate a body-wracking bout of sickness, and I wanted to lie peacefully for a while longer. I lay and listened to my heartbeat, the dawn chorus, and God. And I prayed — prayed that I would not be sick in public, that the baby would be safe, that, when the time came, my waters would not break in the supermarket, or at church, (as my friend's had done)! I prayed that the little unborn child would love the Lord, and be a blessing to us and others. I prayed for all kinds of things as shafts of sunrise shone peacefully, silently, between the curtains.

The memories of two miscarriages, still raw in my mind, unsettled me. Always, at the back of my mind, was the uncertainty of the life of my unborn child. Any minute something could go wrong, and that would be the end of all my hopes again. So I lay there, as I did every morning, almost holding my breath, waiting for a sign of life that would let me know that the tiny being within me had made it through the night as well. I felt a little wriggle — was that the baby? Maybe it was just my stomach mumbling for some muesli. I lay very still, hoping that, if it was the baby, it would move again. Nothing happened. I lay, and thought, and prayed, and listened to a bird singing in the tree outside. Half an hour passed. Bernie was still fast asleep, and the baby was too, it seemed. I hoped . . . I waited and waited. I needed to get up to use the bathroom, but I didn't want to start my day without feeling a flicker of a kick, or the flutter of foetal hand, or even a hearty bounce on my bladder!

The suspense was dreadful. With each passing moment my faith in the little life within was beginning to fade. Finally I could bear it no longer. I felt all over my bump to see if I could feel a part of the baby that was sticking out a bit. Somewhere down my right side I could usually locate a foot. I found something hard, and prodded it gently. 'Come on — wake up!' I prodded a bit harder. Then I felt something wonderful! The baby woke and stretched and turned and wriggled! I felt a thrill as the little life moved within me. I felt a tiny bottom sticking out of my front, and I patted it softly, rolled out of bed, and waddled to the bathroom, feeling at peace with the whole world.

Through all the months of waiting for those dawn movements, and praying in the stillness, I realized that I needed to feel God's Spirit move within me each morning, even more than I needed to feel the baby move. Once I knew that the Spirit was alive in me, I could rise with a song in my heart, content and at peace, to begin a new day.

Sometimes it has been hard to wait in the quiet of the morning and spend time with God. Demanding babies, shrunken or shattering nights, and crazy schedules, have all tried to disrupt those moments of peace and calming contact with the movements of the Spirit. Without those times I soon become frazzled and frustrated, unable to cope so well, fatigued and failing. My ability to cope as a mother has always paralleled the amount of time I have spent with God each day, before I get out of my bed.

Now there are no babies slumbering in my tummy. But still I lie each morning, praying in the quietness, waiting for Someone far greater to stir within me, and bring me His special peace and joy, so I can face the day with confidence.

Dear Father, thank You for the wonderful feeling there is in my life when Your Spirit moves within me. Thank You for strength to live each day with You, and as Your child. Help me to make time to wait in the stillness for You, as each dawn rises. Amen.

Spend some time quietly waiting for the Spirit to move in your life today. Pray as you wait, and listen in the stillness.

Each time you feel the pressures building up on you, pause for a moment and pray for God's strength. Thank Him for helping you, and feel the difference His power can make in your life and in your home.

Away in a manger

I lay in the delivery suite of our local maternity hospital. Our firstborn child lay in my arms, all bathed and clean, and wrapped in a cotton blanket. The room was spotless, white and bright, filled with every latest gadget to relieve pain, and to ease delivery. An empty, transparent crib waited in the corner, the shelves underneath filled with nappies, creams, powders and fresh changes of bedding. I gazed with wonder at the baby I had loved for so long already. I thanked God for a smooth delivery, and for the modern technology that has made having babies so safe. It was not so long ago that childbirth was a life-threatening experience.

Bethany was born a few days into January, and when I was taken to the post-natal ward I noticed the Christmas decorations, still sparkling along the corridors. A wooden crib scene was arranged on a table filled with flowers.

I thought about that other birth, two thousand years ago. I thought of Mary in a smelly stable. No pristine crib with every accessory, just a manger full of hay and some torn rags to swaddle her new-born baby. How terrible! How could God put Mary through such an awful experience?

But then, was it so bad? What was the alternative if Jesus was to be born in Bethlehem, so far from His parents' home? Only an overcrowded inn; people everywhere, no privacy, just mats on the floor wherever they could find a space. And I wondered where I would rather have given birth. I would have wanted somewhere quiet and private, somewhere where I wouldn't have to worry about disturbing others' sleep with my labour pain, somewhere where I could just be alone with my husband, and away from inquisitive eyes and the embarrassment of having to expose my body in public.

The stable was the perfect place. Sheltered, hidden away, peaceful. No worries about making a bit of mess: no one would mind out there, but in the inn it could have been awkward. The hay would make a softer bed than the hard earth floor of the inn. The cries of the baby wouldn't bother anyone, and the manger would make a safe and quiet sleeping place, away from lots of bustling people, with their noise and crush.

And so God knew what was best for Mary. He knew where she would be most comfortable, He knew how to preserve her dignity, He knew where she and the Baby could both find peace. And now I understand why such an apparently inappropriate place was the very best Bethlehem could offer to her King.

Dear Father, thank You for the birth of Jesus. Thank You for the simple beauty, and earthy humility contained in the story of the first Advent. Thank You for the joy and peace and love that it inspires in my life, and help me not to forget the true meaning of His birth on earth. Amen.

Where would you have rather given birth? In the inn, or the stable, or maybe back home in Nazareth?

Think about the special memories you have of your own birthing experiences.

Visit a farm with your children, and show them the stable. Think what it would be like to live there, and share your ideas and feelings about Jesus being born in such a place.

All mine!

Bethany was just a few hours old. Now I was alone with her. All the doctors and nurses had slowly ebbed away. Bernie had had to go and find some sleep. I lay in my bed, and Bethany was sleeping. She was dressed in a little cotton vest with 'Property of Royal Berkshire Hospital' stamped across her chest. The same motif decorated her blankets. She lay in the transparent plastic, fish-tank like cot. I couldn't take my eyes off her. I just lay, somewhat dazed, and gazed at her through the clear plastic. A passing midwife must have noticed the look of rapt wonder on my face, and she said gently, 'Go on; you can pick her up, you know, she's all yours!'

I was afraid to disturb her. If I picked her up she might break, or I might drop her, or something, but I plucked up the courage and picked her out of her cot, carefully, but also somewhat clumsily, and then we nestled down together. I looked at her little red, blotchy face, wisps of damp hair and tiny button nose.

What was I doing with a baby, anyway? I'd hardly even touched one before! I was glad she was a huge nine-pounder. Although she looked tiny to me, she was twice the size of my friend's diminutive four-and-a-half-pound son! But she was still so tiny and wobbly, and I hadn't a clue what to do if she filled her nappy! We'd attended antenatal classes, and learnt how to cope with the birth, which had loomed huge and ominous for months! That behind us, we were now totally clueless, except for the one class I'd attended on breast-feeding!

She is all ours, for always, I thought. For eternity.
Eternity?

Suddenly an important implication of motherhood hit me. Even with nine months to think about it, it was only when I held Bethany in my arms that I began to realize what I had let myself in for! (And eight years later, I'm still finding out!) Bernie and I were to be responsible for guiding this tiny bundle of life into eternity. We were to do all in our power to help her choose to be a part of God's family, forever. True, the final choice would be down to her, but, as parents, we would naturally be the most influential people in her life. For better or worse, for richer, for poorer, in sickness and in health, till death do us part. Incredibly wonderful. Incredibly daunting. The sort of job you only dare consider doing with God to help you.

She screwed up her face, and went all red. I thought she was going to stop breathing. But she filled her nappy instead. I put her back in her crib, and went to fetch some warm water. Well, God, I thought, I'm going to need all the help You can give me! And, to begin with, please give me the courage to change her first nappy!

Dear Father, You are the most experienced Father in the universe! Please help me to know what to do as I care for my children, and guide them towards You and eternity. Thank You for caring for me and my little ones, and for being willing to share Your infinite wisdom with me. Amen.

Think back to those first few precious moments of motherhood, and share your thoughts and feelings at that time.

What have been some of your greatest challenges as a parent, and how has God helped you to face them?

One long, dark, January night

I've never been able to work out why a slightly empty stomach, or a wet nappy, should make a baby yell as much as they do. It really can't be that uncomfortable, can it? Or maybe babies are made to be extra-sensitive to minor discomforts? Maybe it's because yelling is the only way they have to grab an adult's attention? And, when a baby yells, the sound is designed to hit the insanity spot in the brain of any normal, grown-up human being, just to make sure they will do everything possible to make the baby comfortable, and restore some peace. And why not? After all, the baby knows its life is dependent on encouraging any convenient adult to submit to its immediate demands.

When I had my first baby I noticed something that really amused me. Every time Bethany cried in someone else's arms, she would be swiftly handed back to Mummy. And someone would usually say, 'That's the best thing about other people's babies, you can always hand them back when they cry!' Young and inexperienced as I was, I felt like telling them that I probably had no more idea than they had how to make her stop crying! A feed, a nappy change, a fingertip of teething gel, a few pats on the back to bring up a bubble, that was my complete repertoire of infant remedies. But sometimes the problem would be some other, obscure discomfort that would linger disturbingly for hours, or dissolve into sleep before I'd figured out what it was.

When Bethany was born we lived in a little country

town which still had an old maternity home. Bethany was delivered in the city hospital, and the next day Bernie drove me to the quiet and cosy cottage hospital. I had the luxury of being able to stay there for up to a week, so I planned to make the most of it. My friend was in the next bed with her baby girl, and we had lots of time to chat, shed a tear at the frustrations of feeding, giggle about little things, and be pampered by having our meals cooked for us, and nurses on hand if we had any problems.

Finally the last night came. Bethany had been quite a contented little thing until then. She fed and slept well, and wasn't too much bother, and by the end of the week I was beginning to get the hang of how to change her messy nappies. But that last night she would not settle. She wriggled and whimpered, and then bawled and bawled. I tried feeding her, but she didn't want to know. It was getting on for midnight and I was exhausted from the struggle, but nothing would soothe her into the serenity of sleep. I felt sorry for the three other mums and their babies who had the misfortune of sharing our room. I was embarrassed, and feeling more helpless and stupid by the minute.

Finally a nurse swept me into a side room. 'Come on! Change her — do something like that — she'll be happy then!' The sweet, Chinese nurse was trying to help, but I was all thumbs, and numb with tiredness. The tapes wouldn't stick, and Bethany wriggled and yelled the whole time. I began to feel discouraged about the whole idea of motherhood — it was then about two o'clock, and everything in the world always seems blacker that time of night. The thought of going home, and being on my own with this unhappy little scrap of life scared me crazy. I thought I would never cope. After all, what use was I as a mother if I couldn't pacify my own baby?

I tried feeding her again, and suddenly she threw up . . . and threw up . . . and threw up. I had never seen so much vomit. Now both she and I needed a bath and a change — would this nightmare never end? Where was sleep when I needed it? The nurse left me, and I struggled dimly and clumsily to clean up all the mess, sheer exhaustion crushing painfully through my head. 'Oh, no!' I thought, 'now she'll need feeding all over again!' I imagined I'd be up for another hour, feeding, bringing up bubbles, changing another nappy — and there was always the possibility she might throw up again, and I had no more fresh clothes.

I climbed into bed and held her damp, sad little body, and prayed for strength. I felt so alone, so fragile. The world seemed somehow big and dark and scary. But even before I managed to feed her, her body relaxed into sleep. I laid her gently in the plastic hospital crib, kissed her little fuzzy head, and crashed into blissful oblivion. Just then I was too tired to realize the touch of a loving Father, who knew I'd reached my limits. But I'd thank Him in the morning.

It was the next morning, too, when I realized all my trouble had been caused by an overindulgence in mango nectar, a gift from a friend. I'd drunk a litre in two or three hours! It was so delicious, and refreshing, and, after nine months of nauseating pregnancy, it was wonderful to taste fruit properly again. Obviously mango-flavoured breast milk didn't agree with Bethany's neonatal stomach on that long, dark, January night, but, funnily enough, mango has been her favourite fruit ever since!

Joel stands in his crib and wails when he wakes. But as soon as he is picked up, and can feel me close, he is quiet and happy again. It warms me right through to feel that I can turn his tears into smiles, just by being there, and hugging him. If he's hurt or very upset, then it's almost the most wonderful thing in the world to hold him, whisper in his ear, and snuggle down with him under our patchwork quilt, until his face is full of those cheeky little grins again. I am his mum, and sometimes I am the only person in the world who can comfort his sad little heart, and fill him with peace after an awkward fall, or the shock of unexpected pain.

It is wonderful to be there for a child when his whole world seems scary and dark, or lonely and big; to kiss a tear-smudged face, and wipe the blood from a grubby knee; to hold a child who's crying, and doesn't know why; to comfort, to be there, to make the world a friendlier-feeling place and whisper words of love and encouragement. Those moments of closeness and comfort warm my heart as well as theirs. And when I'm the one who's sad and broken, and the world caves in on me, I know there is Someone to hold me, too, and whisper words of hope. Someone to blow away the scary bits, and hold my hand. My world feels so much better because I know He's always there.

Dear Father, thank You that You delight to comfort me. Thank You that when it all gets too much, I can crawl into Your arms and feel Your loving promises chase away all the scary things, and the things that hurt and make me bleed. Help me to be gentle with the children that need comforting so many times through a busy day. I'm glad You know how much I can bear, and that You are strong enough to bear everything for me. Amen.

How does God comfort you?

List some special texts and promises that He whispers to you when you are feeling fragile.

Aim to share one of those texts with another mother this week. Write it in a pretty card, or on a bookmark, and send it as a little gift to lift her up, too.

Keep a note of the different ways God has comforted you in your life, in special situations, or just from day to day.

The mother on the mountain

Nothing moves me like the story of a mother. I can listen to reports of news from all around the world, and sense scraps of the horror being inflicted and suffered in a thousand different ways, but stories of individual suffering reach right through to my heart. My father worked for the relief organization ADRA, and he has driven truck-loads of aid into Sarajevo. He met a young mother, trapped there with two little daughters. I have read one of her letters, heard about her struggles for survival, and now, every time I hear about something happening in that ravaged city, I wonder how it is affecting her and her family, and I pray for their safety.

My heart aches for mothers whose children die in tragic circumstances; mothers whose children are missing; or murdered. My vivid imagination enters a little into their world, and pictures how it would be for me.

One evening, several years ago, long lines of weary, broken people walked across my television screen, each carrying a few belongings tied in a sheet or old sack. The Kurdish refugees were fleeing Iraq. Pregnant women were giving birth by the side of the road, then having to get up and carry on walking. In the refugee camps people were already dying because of inadequate food, warmth, water and sanitation. Mothers rocked their tiny, starving, sick children, giving a last bit of comfort. The situation was desperate. It was breaking my heart that mothers and children were suffering like that, and there was nothing I could do.

The news report ended and I sat, alone, in the quiet of the evening, and just felt. I felt all kinds of strange feelings. I put myself in the situation of those Kurdish mothers, trying to do their best for their children. I tasted a little of their salty tears, imagined their breaking hearts as they watched their little ones suffer, and even die. 'Dear Father, what can I do for them? I feel so helpless here. Nothing I can do can make a difference to their lives right now, when they need so much help. How can I show I care?'

As I sat in the stillness I seemed to hear a voice say, 'You can pray. I want you to pray for one particular mother out there on that hillside. Her little child is very sick, and she doesn't know what to do. Just pray for her. And I will hear your prayers.'

And so I prayed, and prayed, and felt a sense of peace. I was doing the only thing I could do, and it was more than a few pennies in a charity box, or a piece of clothing, or a tin of beans. It was being part of a channel of love from heaven to earth — tapping the greatest resource in the universe.

Out there on the hillside . . . what happened? I may never know. Maybe a mother felt strengthened and comforted; maybe a little child was given some medicine and food by an aid worker; maybe the child fell asleep, and woke with the fever gone . . . I don't know, and it doesn't matter. It was enough to reach out through the night, with a prayer and God's love, and share the burden of a suffering mother.

Dear Father, thank You for the gift of prayer. Thank You that when I feel so inadequate to help in any human way, I can take hold of Your hand in prayer, and be a channel of Your power and love to a suffering world. Amen.

Whenever you hear the news reports, pray for the mothers whose lives have been affected by the events of the day. Try to make your prayers as specific as you can. Think of their special needs and concerns; pray that their strength will continue, that they will be given wisdom to make good choices in difficult circumstances, and pray that, somehow, through it all, they may know more of God's love.

Dc something practical this week to help a suffering mother somewhere in the world.

Foxes, phobias and faith

For months we had had problems trying to get Bethany to sleep at night. She was nearing 2, and I was tired of the struggle each evening. It was obvious she was afraid of something.

Every evening we would read a Bible story, and pray together. We would pray especially that Bethany wouldn't be afraid, and that her guardian angel would be close and watch over her during the night. I would sing 'Turn your eyes upon Jesus' to her, because I could never remember the words of any lullabies. I would hold her hand and, when I thought she was asleep, I would try to slip away quietly. But, more often than not, she would wake up, and we'd start all over again. I'd read all about just saying goodnight and leaving the child to scream herself to sleep, but I couldn't face it. She was so scared that it didn't seem fair to increase her fears. We couldn't imagine why she was so terrified.

We would talk to her about her evening fears, and try to find out what was going on, but she couldn't identify why she was afraid. She was still young, and the emotion of fear was much stronger than her ability to express her feelings. Her fear seemed even stranger because she was generally a confident, secure little girl.

One night, as I sat by her bed and held her hand, she whispered, 'Mummy, I'm afraid of the foxes.'

'The foxes?' I whispered back. 'What is it that makes you scared about the foxes?'

'I'm afraid they will come in the night and eat me up.'

'But, Bethany, the doors are all locked, and Mummy is here all the time. I wouldn't let a fox get into the house, and, anyway, a fox would be much more scared of us.'

'No, I know they can get me.' She was insistent.

Well, at least we knew a bit more about the fear. We tried everything we could to help put her little mind at rest. But one morning we opened the curtains to find a fox looking at us through a window which overlooked a field. It stared at us for one moment, then it turned tail and fled into the buttercups and tall grass. That experience didn't do much to encourage her!

OK, we knew she was afraid of foxes, but why? Finally, the penny dropped. Months before, when Bethany was only just one, she had heard Granny talking. Now Granny keeps chickens at the bottom of her garden. One night a fox had found its way into the chicken run and killed a bird, barely waiting to leave the area before having its dinner. Bethany had been within earshot of this conversation, and understood that:

a. foxes come in the night, and,

b. they kill things, and eat them!

Armed with only these two scraps of information she had a right to be afraid of foxes!

Once we understood what had happened we were able to explain to Bethany why foxes kill chickens, and how the fox got into Granny's chicken run. Slowly she began to realize that she did not need to be afraid of foxes in the night because they can't get into houses, and they don't like eating little girls! Within a week she was able to go off to sleep by herself each night.

Fears are funny things. Some fear is good, and we need it for our own protection and well-being. Fear can be a type of internal 'guardian angel'. But some fears come about because we don't know all the facts. Or from strange childhood experiences. Or sometimes they are just 'there' and we don't know why, but we struggle to live with them anyway. Often our fears are irrational and ludicrous, and even when we know the truth they linger on, still haunting us, and disrupting our lives.

God wants us to be free from our irrational fears. I'm glad He's there, holding our hand in the night, and trying to bring us peace and comfort as a Father at our bedside, till one day we will understand that there is nothing left to fear.

Dear Father, thank You for the way that fear can help me to avoid dangers, and protect others. Thank You that You love me, and You want me to be free from my irrational, disabling fears. Please help me to overcome them. Strengthen me and bring me Your peace and courage to face the stressful situations in my life. Thank You. Amen.

What things are you afraid of? Are your fears irrational, or are they helpful, because they encourage you to take good, healthy precautions?

List your fears, under two headings, 'irrational' and 'helpful', and think about why these things make you feel afraid. Then read Isaiah 41:10.

Pray for courage to overcome your disabling fears, and thank God for the victory He has given you over them.

Pyjama prayer

Bethany was still quite small; it was before Nathan was born, and I was trying to get her ready for bed. Like many children she was able to find extra reserves of energy which have to be burned up in the last half an hour before bedtime, just when my own energy quota for the day has finally given out. So there we were in the bathroom, she was going off like a firecracker, and I was like a spent sparkler. Trying to get her into a nappy and pyjamas was like trying to gift-wrap a live rabbit! I was coming to the end of my tether, and she was boisterous and mischievous.

I was exhausted, yet again! It must have showed, I know I was finding it hard to be patient and I probably yelled a bit. Bethany hid in the shower cubicle and, as I tried to catch her, I knocked over a bottle of shampoo that had come adrift from its lid. Thick, slippery liquid trickled onto the carpet — a trivial thing, but the last straw. I finally caught hold of Bethany with the intention of forcefully manhandling her into her nightclothes, when she suddenly stopped. 'Mummy, I want to pray,' she said. Prayers normally wait till after the pyjama performance. Was she trying delaying tactics? Was this some more mischief? If I said 'No', would it stunt her spiritual growth? Who am I to say a child can't pray if she wants to? After a moment's thought I decided to give her the benefit of the doubt. 'All right,' I said, 'what would you like to say?' 'I want to pray that you'll be a nice mummy!' she said!

I was temporarily stunned. Then I saw the funny side of it all! I laughed and laughed, and forgot I was so tired. Bethany laughed too. Then I let her pray, 'Please God, make my Mummy be nice, and not grouchy. Thank You, Amen.' She giggled her way into her nightclothes with very little fuss. We had a big, warm hug together. I read her a story, and it was prayer-time again. 'Thank You God for making my Mummy nice again. She's very nice really, only she gets a bit grouchy when she's tired. Please forgive her. Amen'

I tucked her under her quilts, and gave her one last kiss. She smiled at me. 'I'm glad God answered my prayer,' she whispered. 'You're lovely when you're nice.' Her eyelids were finally drooping their lashes over her peach-bloom cheeks.

I tiptoed out of the room, and turned out the light.

'Yes, Father, I, too, thank You for answering her prayer. Forgive me for being tired and grouchy with her, and help me to be nice more often. Amen.'

Dear Father, sometimes I am so tired, and I feel so cross inside. Please fill me with Your love and peace, so that there isn't room for the grouchies inside me. And please, above all, help me to be a nice Mummy, because the ones I love the most need to have the best bits of me, and not the worst bits. Thank You for helping me. Amen.

What tends to give you the grouchies? Can you plan to avoid these situations by getting to sleep earlier, or organizing your time better?

It's a strange anomaly that those we love the most usually see us at our worst, and those we hardly know tend to see us at our best! What can we do to be the best and 'nicest' for those we love, as well as for others?

How can you help your little children learn to pray to Jesus on their own, throughout the day, when they need help, when they are scared, when they are happy, as well as at bedtimes and worship times?

-

The toddler and the two laws

Bethany wandered into the living room with a piece of scrap paper in her hand. She was not quite 2 years old and she enjoyed scribbling and pretending to write. 'Here you are, Mummy,' she said. 'This is for everyone in the world.' I looked up from the cross-stitch sampler I was working on, trying to remember my place on the pattern.

'Oh, that's nice, darling,' I said, with a quick glance at her hieroglyphics, then back to the pink thread.

'Yes', she said, 'it's very important. It tells everyone what they need to do.'

'Oh, does it?' I said, doubtfully.

'Yes,' she said, emphatically, 'look!' She demanded my full attention; I gave up on the sampler.

'See,' she said. 'On this side it says that everyone must love God and obey Him, and on this side it says that everyone must hate Satan. They are the two most important things for everyone to know.'

I nearly fell off my chair. Here was my little toddler preaching to the world! This was what she felt was the most important thing to tell everyone. How many adults could sum up the facts of eternal life so clearly? This was nothing we had taught her directly, just what she had realized herself, from the Bible stories we had told her, from watching our lives, listening to us talk about God, and being part of our prayer-times. I don't know exactly how it happened, but I know she could under-stand those things only because God was working on her heart. We weren't 'on our own' as we tried to share God with our children; He was there too, helping them comprehend, through the friendship of His Holy Spirit.

She handed me the piece of paper and went back to scribble something else, blissfully unaware of her innocent profundity, while I folded the paper for my treasure box, and tucked another special moment into my heart.

Dear Father, thank You for revealing Yourself to our children. Thank You for the truths that they can help us understand. Amen.

Think of some times when your children have surprised you with their understanding of spiritual things.

If you were to sum up what you believe as a Christian in two sentences, what would you say?

Ask your children to tell you why it is important to love Jesus, and listen to what they say.

Lost and found

Our town still has one of those old-fashioned markets with little stalls piled high with fruit and vegetables, and the vendors calling out their best deals, each one clamouring for our attention and our money. It is a busy, bustling, noisy sort of place to go, and there's always lots to see as barrow-loads of fresh stuff wind their way through the crowds to restock the colourful stalls.

Bernie went there with Bethany one Friday to buy our fresh food for the following week. My mother was staying with us, and she went to shop at the large supermarket across the street from the market. Bernie had almost finished when he noticed some particularly beautiful grapes. He stopped to choose a bunch, and then stood in line to pay for it. He handed over the coins, and reached out again for Bethany's hand. She was a tiny $2\frac{1}{2}$-year-old, not even as tall as the stall tables; and as Bernie reached out his hand hit empty air. His heart flipped. A sickening, body-crunching fear gripped at his chest: that heavy, desperate dread you feel when you realize your child is lost. He began to search among the crowds and stalls. It was truly like looking for a needle in a haystack. She was tiny, and pretty, and there were a thousand different places she could be. And worse still, it was the easiest place in the world to abduct a child.

My mother finished her shopping, loaded it into the car, and thought she'd try to find Bernie while she waited. She found him, still frantically looking, asking around if anyone had seen a little girl with pig-tails and pink shorts. No one had. He went back to the grape stall again, with the desperate hope that she might have gone back there. We'd always told her that if she got lost, she should go back to the place where she last remembered seeing us.

'Have you seen a little girl, so-high, pink shorts, hair in pig-tails?' Bernie's words were breathless and frantic. He was in a hurry. Only the day before he'd witnessed the birth of his little son, Nathan, and he was due, right then, to collect us from the hospital. But he couldn't go until he'd found Bethany. There is never a good time to lose a child, but this must have been one of the worst. My mother had visions of Bernie having to call the police, and then having to go to the maternity hospital to tell me that Bethany was lost. She worried about the effect the news would have on me. Appalling news at any time, made ten times worse by the fragile emotional state of a post-natal mother!

'Yer lost a kid?' someone asked. 'Yer wanna check ol' Smithson's apple stall. He collects lost kids. Sits 'em up on his ol' barrow, gives 'em an apple. Anyone gets lost here, that's where you'll find 'em. Up there on the left. Can't miss it.'

And there she sat, munching a bright red apple, calmly telling people that her father had gone and left her, and her mother was in the hospital getting a little brother. 'Poor abandoned and unwanted child!' they must have thought. 'Whatever is the world coming to!'

Only a parent can know the relief that comes when a lost child is found. Some may scold a bit; some may burst into tears, but inside there is just sheer happiness. Our little lost one has been found, the ache and the agony of separation is over, and we're all together again.

I love the picture of the father in the story of the prodigal son. His son is lost, terribly lost. Anything could have happened. He's been gone for months. But still the father is out there, looking up the road, every day, waiting and watching, longing and looking. And one day he spots his son, a tiny dishevelled figure limping down the lane, in such a mess he can be smelt a long way off, too. But that doesn't matter. His son is back. It doesn't matter where he's been, or what he's done. No blame, no punishment, no 'I told you so's'. Just love and compassion, happiness, and a welcome place at home again. The past is behind them. Tomorrow is another day, and a good place to start over, together, again.

Dear Father, thank You that whenever I may wander away from You, You are always waiting, hoping and looking for me to come back home. Help me to realize that the most exciting, beautiful, happy and loving place I can be is at home with You. Help me to make my home and my church a welcoming place for others, where they can be touched by Your love. Amen.

Think about a time when you or your children were lost. How did you feel? What was it like to be reunited?

Think of something you can do today to make your home a more welcoming place for your children.

Think about something you can do to help someone at your church feel more welcome. Especially think about reaching out to another mother.

When God helps with the housework

God cares about the little things in my life. I know He does. He cares for those little things that seem almost insignificant to other people, but make a great difference to my efficiency and sanity as a busy mum. He is aware of the tiny fragments of my life that no one else even thinks about. As I hurriedly stuff a dark load into the washing machine He often reminds me to check the pockets for paper tissues. Even when I think I've checked already, or I feel I can't be bothered, I look, and when God has reminded me there's always at least one lurking somewhere.

When I go shopping, He may whisper, 'You need to buy some extra spaghetti sauce this week.' And when I go to look for a jar it is on extra special offer, so I take several. The next day there is a telephone call and some friends have decided to come over for lunch.

One day I was up to my neck in housework and children, but I found myself making a huge dish of lasagne. Bernie walked into the kitchen as I poured tomato sauce over the pasta strips. 'What are you doing that for? I thought you were really busy today!'

'I don't know. Something inside is telling me to do this, for some reason.'

Dinner was already made, so I popped the lasagne into the freezer for another time.

Two days later we had a phone call from someone who needed a will to be signed before the family took their amazing, ancient, converted Jeep on the ferry from our town to France. Their pastor was away, and couldn't sign the document, so they wondered if they could come by quickly to see us, as we lived close by the ferry terminal. As I put the phone down I realized the caller was an old friend of mine from summer camp. Now we were both married, and we hadn't recognized each other's names!

Sue arrived with her husband, baby daughter and brother-in-law. They had hours before the ferry was due in, so I invited them to stay, slipped the lasagne into the microwave to defrost, and thanked God for speaking to me, even though I hadn't realized it was He at the time!

Now I see that God is helping me in a hundred little ways. I thank Him for helping me to choose a shopping trolley with straight wheels, so I don't have to do battle with a wayward one. I thank Him for helping me to notice the sale items and save a few extra pennies on things we really need. I thank God when He opens up a fresh checkout, just as I arrive, so I don't have to wait in line with three tired children.

Once I found an ink stain on Bernie's best shirt. I tried all kinds of stain removal, and nothing seemed to shift it. I left it on the kitchen counter. Discouraged and frustrated, I prayed, 'Dear Father, I don't know what to do here. We can't afford another shirt at the moment, and Bernie needs it for church. Please help me. Thank You. Amen.' Just a quick prayer, a brief connection with the most powerful Stain Remover in the universe. I went upstairs to straighten out the bedrooms, and when I came back down, the shirt was a spotless white.

Sometimes He may remind me to check that the back gate is closed so our lop-eared rabbit, and baby Jojo, can run around the garden in safety. Once He reminded me to put an extra outfit in the nappy bag. For months I hadn't bothered to take along spare clothes for Joel. He'd not been messy for ages, so I stopped bothering. I popped a spare pair of overalls and a sweater in with the nappies. The next day, at church, a friend's baby managed to ruin all his clothes with one runny nappy. She had nothing to put on him, so we loaned him the sweater and the overalls, and they came in useful after all!

Whenever anything goes smoothly and easily, or God reminds me to do something that makes a positive difference in my housework schedule, or that helps me to keep the children safe and happy, I try to take the time to thank Him for caring for me. Now I've begun to notice just how much help God gives me with the housework, I try to listen for His voice, to ask His advice more often. And the God who controls the whole universe, and patterns the stars, also numbers my hairs, and He lets me know that nothing in my life is too small to be beyond His loving care.

Dear Father, thank You for caring about the infinite minutiae of my hectic life. These little things matter to You because they matter to me. Thank You for all the help You have given me. Be with me today as I clean and cook and launder and do all the 'mummy' kinds of things. Thank You for everything, Amen.

List all the jobs you have to do today, and pray about each one before you even start to do anything. At the end of the day, think about all the ways God has helped you.

Imagine Jesus' coming to your home. What would He do? It would be lovely to sit at His feet and just listen to Him, or to pour out your heart into His loving one. But He knows you have to care for the children, too, and make the dinner, and wash the clothes, and maybe rush to the shops. Do you think He would just sit, or do you think He would involve Himself in helping you? Maybe He would take the children for a walk in the country and show them His creation. Maybe He'd help sort laundry, or make you a delicious meal of fruits and nuts, with flavours from heaven. Imagine what He would do if He shared this day with you. And how might Jesus' being there change your focus for the day?

And then, remember, He is always there, and He always cares, because He loves you.

Beating the blues

No matter what our lives are like there are times when we can all feel a bit down or fed up. Long winters, dull days, fatigue, work pressures, loneliness and challenging circumstances can all take their toll on our physical, emotional and spiritual health. But there are lots of things we can do to help brighten our lives when they feel particularly dull. Rather than reaching for some tablets, or a bottle, and yelling at the kids again, try some of these ideas!

Try a day drinking only water, and eating only fruits, vegetables and nuts. This can help clear up a sluggish system, and give you extra energy and vitality. If you like, try doing this one day a week.

Climb up a nearby hill; take lots of deep breaths, then run down again, and imagine you are flying!

Try a new hobby. Go to an evening class, or find a book in the library to help you get started. Or go to a craft shop and choose a kit. Try to choose something that you will be able to manage easily, and that will not take too long, so you will soon have a finished result about which you will feel good.

Want to go shopping, but don't have much money? Make a list of all the cards you need to buy for birthdays and special events throughout the next few months. Then visit all the card shops in town, looking for the most appropriate greetings. Buy as many as you can afford. You will have fun reading the funny verses, and finding cards that will suit your friends perfectly. If you have time, write the cards, address and stamp the envelopes, and write posting dates on them in pencil. Pile them up in order with the nearest birthday on the top, and they'll be ready just when you need them!

Find a skipping rope, and see how many jumps you can do without stopping. Or borrow a bike, and find an area of safe cycle paths to ride around. Exercise releases chemicals into your body which can help you feel happier.

Go out in the garden and blow a whole tub of bubbles. See how big you can blow your bubbles. The deep, slow, breathing control needed to make large bubbles will help your body to feel relaxed. The children can join in the fun, too, blowing bubbles and chasing them around the garden.

Make a list of all the things in your life for which you are thankful. If you feel particularly stuck for ideas, start with 'air so I can breathe'! Don't stop until you've written at least twenty things on your list!

Volunteer some of your time for a project for homeless people, disabled adults or children, or elderly people. This way you can meet new people, help others, and realize how fortunate you are. If possible, try to volunteer on a regular basis, as you can be more effective if you are familiar with the people you are helping, and the work you have to do. Maybe the whole family could take part in a volunteer project, such as a soup run, or visiting nursing homes.

Invite your spouse to do something special with you. Go on a picnic together; go to a concert or art show. See how many things you can do in your town without having to spend any money.

Write a letter to a family member you haven't seen for a while. Even better, go and visit him or her, and plan a special surprise.

Fresh flowers in the house can really cheer you up. Buy a bunch, or pick a tiny posy of daisies. Better still, find someone with whom to share your flowers, so you can help to brighten another home, too.

Bake a batch of your favourite cookies, cakes, or bread, and give some away to a neighbour.

Do something to improve your environment. Repaint a small room; sort out a messy cupboard, clean and polish your car. The job may not be exciting, but you'll feel better once it's done. If you can, do a less pleasant job with someone else, then you will have more fun, and be better motivated.

Dress the children in old clothes. Find a pair of thick rubber gloves for each person, and a large plastic bag. Go to a favourite place which is often spoiled by dropped litter, and help to make it more beautiful.

Find an old catalogue and count all the things you *wouldn't* want to have; things that are unnecessary, things you don't like, things that would take up too much space, or mean extra work. Then be glad you haven't got any of them!

Flick through the catalogue again, and choose the presents you would like to give your friends and family, if only you had the money! You could even involve the whole family in the fun! Cut out the 'gifts' you have chosen, and give one to each person in your family, saying why you'd like to be able to give them that particular gift.

Dear Father, thank You that You always love us, even when we feel tired and down. Thank You that there are lots of fun things to do that are healthy and caring, and that can cheer our hearts. Thank You for bearing all our cares. Amen.

Try doing at least one of the above ideas next time you feel down.

Find a Bible and read John 3:16, putting your name in the

gaps to personalize the message. Then rewrite it in your own words. For example:

For God loved Karen so much that He gave His one and only Son to die in her place, so that if Karen will believe in Him, she will not die, but she will live with Him forever, in heaven.

Thank God that He loves you that much, no matter how you feel!

Feasting on the Father

I never really thought much about how I would feed my babies. I hoped I would be able to breast-feed them myself; all the fuss about sterilizing bottles, and making up feeds put me off the alternatives. It seemed so much easier to have milk 'on tap', pre-heated, sterile, and always with me! Besides, if I didn't have to hold a bottle for the baby, then I could arrange things so I had two hands free to type on my laptop computer! How convenient! A happy baby, and a happy mum, and a few extra pennies along the way, hopefully!

There are times when I love nursing my babies. It's sweet to hold them close as they stroke my hair, or gaze up at me with the one big eye I can see, and occasionally smile through a suck. It's great to feel so wanted, to be so much in demand, to be the only person who can feed my children, so no one can take them away from me for long! Feeding them makes me stop and sit still for a while, and take a refreshing break, to read, type, or even sew.

But there are the odd times, in the middle of the night, or during a particularly busy day, or when I'm ill, when a constantly sucking child almost drives me bananas! Sometimes I have had to let Bernie take over a screaming child while I let my body have a rest — you can have too much of a good thing!

It's lovely to watch an infant with its mother. Throughout the day the baby needs to be fed over and over, especially if it is being fed 'on demand.' He or she needs nourishment from the mother, closeness, comfort and satisfaction. The baby may even yell first, to make the mother pay attention to its needs. The infant knows what it wants, and is determined to get it. And why not? After all, its life depends on it! It's only by feeding on something that a baby can be strong, healthy and happy, and keep on growing. Once it stops feeding, it will be very miserable and sick, and will lose weight.

I've learned a little more about the way I should relate to God from nursing my babies. Just as they need me to be there all the time, I need God. They need to drink often, and deeply, till they are satisfied, just as I should come to God often, and feast on what He has to offer me, until I am filled with His Spirit. I need comfort from God and closeness with Him, and I am sure He is thrilled when I metaphorically rest in His arms, all at peace, and smile up at Him in my joy.

Dear Father, thank You for always being there to satisfy my every need, to comfort me, and to be close to me. Help me to come to You often and drink deeply from all that You have to offer, so that I can be strong and healthy as I grow in You. Amen.

How can you be 'nursed' by God?

How can you find time to come to God often, throughout the day, when you are so busy?

Stick an encouraging text or prayer reminder on the bathroom mirror, or the refrigerator door. Pause each time you see the text, and memorize the words, think about them and pray that you will receive fresh insights into their meaning.

Fishflakes in the soup

I was making soup again. Soup is one of the most helpful
things known to a mother, especially if she can whizz it
all smooth in a blender and disguise lots of otherwise
offensive vegetables, like peas, and carrots, spinach and
onions. It is also quick and simple; it's a meal in itself,
with a hunk of bread; it makes very little dish-washing;
and it uses up lots of left-overs. I'm also quite happy to
serve a pot of soup and some home-made bread to any
guests that come to visit.

This time I was making soup for Bernie to take along
and share with some other church members. They were
going to be standing outside a supermarket mall all day,
collecting money for mission work. It was early spring,
and still quite chilly, and Bernie was going to come home
and collect the hot soup and bread for their midday snack.

Bethany was 'helping' me. She was about 3, and she sat
on the kitchen counter. I would put some salt in her hand,
or some herbs, and she would have fun throwing it into
the pot. The door bell rang, and I went to answer it. I chatted a few minutes, then went back to the kitchen. Bethany
was still sitting on the counter. 'Mummy! I've been helping! Look, I put some of this in the soup, too!'

I did look, and my heart sank. In her hand she held a
little round pot that looked exactly like a pot of herbs,
except that it wasn't. It was food for our goldfish. Dried
flakes of something that smelled very fishy indeed! I
looked into the pot. Most of the flakes were still clinging

to the surface, and I tried to scoop them up with a spoon. I knew I couldn't be sure I had them all.

The situation might not have been so bad if all the helpers were fish-eaters anyway! But they weren't. They were all vegetarian! Bernie was arriving in a few minutes; there was no time to make more soup. I hoped I'd removed most, if not all, of the fish food, and blended the remains with a few extra herbs to try to mask any odd aromas.

I wonder about God. I wonder how many times God has let me 'help' Him, sitting like a child, scattering oregano, while He has been doing the real work. So often I feel good about what I think I'm doing to help, when my greatest contribution has really only been adding the herbs to His ready-made soup. And I wonder how often I've inadvertently added the wrong 'ingredients' in my eagerness to be helpful, and made a complete mess of things, so that God has had to spend time putting it all right again?

I don't know. And I guess I won't, till heaven. But spooning fish-flakes out of lentil soup, I stopped, and wondered, and suddenly felt very small in it all.

Dear Father, thank You for letting me 'help' You, not because You need me, but rather because I need You, and it is exciting and fun to be a part of what You have to do in this world. Please give me wisdom so that I don't put metaphorical fish-flakes in Your perfect soup! Amen.

What are some positive ways of responding to a child who is 'only trying to help' but ends up making extra work?!

Next time a child makes a mistake, try telling him or her that you make mistakes too, and try to be that little bit more patient, remembering God is having to be patient with you, as well!

Prayerfully consider what you can do today that will really help God.

Watcher in the night

I remember feeling the effects of maternal fatigue syndrome. I was exhausted. Nathan had just turned one and he was very mobile. When he couldn't toddle fast enough, he went down on all fours and raced like a turbo-charged chipmunk. He went over the floor like a vacuum cleaner — anything he found in his path disappeared into his mouth. I could keep the floors fairly clean and tidy inside, but the garden was a different matter. Stones, grass, flowers and earth — anything that he could grab was stuffed into his little face. Stones went in dirty and came out gleaming. I had even caught him when he was feasting on rabbit droppings after he had managed to open the hutch door. I had to watch him every moment. He was at the stage when nothing was safe. He climbed like a squirrel. He got into everything. He could create an earthquake zone in one minute flat.

As if my having to watch him every minute of the day wasn't bad enough, he didn't sleep very well. He woke at 5.30am, which wouldn't have been so bad if he'd not also woken at 12.04am, 1.45am, and 3.15am. When he woke he would yell for ages. We tried leaving him to yell, to see if he would yell himself back to sleep, but he could yell for two hours or more without letting up, and at the end was more awake than when he started. When it all got too much, I climbed into bed with Bethany!

I could feel my nerves fraying at the edges. Some days I felt as if I were disintegrating. I couldn't concentrate. I was even too tired to speak properly. I had no time on my own without at least one child to watch over. I'd had little more than five hours' sleep a night for months, and it was taking its toll on my physical, emotional and spiritual health. I knew I was supposed to get adequate sleep to be healthy; I was desperate for sleep, but there was no time to catch up on sleep during the day with two toddlers to care for and a husband who, as a pastor, was out most evenings. I could understand why sleep deprivation was used by the Japanese as a form of torture.

Then, in the middle of a very black night, after a session of Nathan's yelling and a particularly stressful day of intense mothering, I'd had enough. 'Father, please help me! Do something! I can't go on like this much longer! Do You know what it's like to be a mother, and watch children almost twenty-four hours a day, and keep them from hurting themselves; to be there to fill their every need, listen to their screams in the night? Do You know what it's like? Do You care? Are You listening?'

My heart yelled the angry words into the velvet night. And when I was done, I lay exhausted and listened to the Spirit within.

'Karen, yes, I am here. I've been watching My children for several thousand years, and now I have millions of them to keep an eye on. And you wouldn't believe the scrapes they get themselves into! It wouldn't be so bad if the worst things they ever did were to eat rabbit droppings, and scribble on the wallpaper! I haven't had a wink of sleep in all those years. There are always thousands of them wanting My attention at once. I listen for their cries in the night, and I hear each one, just as I've heard you. It's hard work; believe Me; I know. But I love them all just the same. I'm glad when they cry out for Me. At least they still need Me. And while any of them need Me, I'll be there to pick them up, hug them, wipe their tears, and listen to their sadnesses, because I'm their Father, and their Mother. I'm all that many of them have. And I know it won't last forever. The day will come when there won't be any more wayward ones to watch, or cries in the night. The relief will be universal! But in the meantime you need some sleep, so off you go, and let Me do the watching for the night, since I'm up anyway.'

Dear Father, thank You for being awake, even when I am asleep. Thank You for watching in the night. Thank You that You are always there, and that You always care. Amen.

What have you learned about God's loving care while being a mum?

As you go to bed tonight, think about God, awake and watching forever, and drift off to sleep with a sense of peace, knowing that you can trust Him to care for you, and your family, all through the night.

The next time you tell God just how you are feeling, don't forget to think about His side of the story too!

'Dear Jesus, thank You . . . '

I love to listen to children pray. Their words are so simple and straightforward.

I remember when Nathan first managed to pray. That day he had been given a special toy, one that he'd wanted for a long time — a Thomas the Tank Engine train. If you don't know about Thomas the Tank Engine, he is a cheeky little engine featured in a delightful series of children's books, written by an Anglican vicar. The books are designed to explain how the old railways and steam trains used to work, but the stories also teach children the importance of unselfishness, humility, politeness, friendship and forgiveness, in a warm and gentle manner.

Well, Nathan was delighted with his new, shiny, blue engine. When he pulled it backwards, the motor wound up, and then the engine would rush forward across the room. It was great fun, and we all got down on the floor and zoomed the engine back and forth, on a cobweb of imaginary train lines.

At prayer time, Nathan managed one of his very first prayers: 'Dear Jesus, thank You for Thomas the Tank Engine, Amen.' We were delighted that at last he had started to pray his own little prayers. At supper-time Nathan offered to pray again. This was wonderful, we thought. We bowed our heads and folded our hands, and waited for Nathan . . . 'Dear Jesus, thank You for Thomas the Tank Engine, Amen.' At bedtime he wanted to pray too: 'Dear Jesus, thank You for Thomas the Tank Engine, Amen.'

In fact, there probably isn't another toy on earth that has been so thankfully received. Try as we might, we couldn't get Nathan to pray anything else. For months, when he prayed before a meal, it was: 'Dear Jesus, thank You for Thomas the Tank Engine, Amen.' Then one of us would prompt him softly, 'And what else? . . . ' 'Oh, yes, and thank You for our food, Amen.'

After several months, Nathan learned to say, 'Dear Jesus, thank You for our food, Amen.' We were thrilled that months of effort had finally paid off . . . . But for the next six months all he could pray was, 'Dear Jesus, thank You for the food, Amen.' This was his worship prayer, meal-time prayer, bedtime prayer, and prayer before travelling.

Finally he managed to include some variety in his celestial communications, and now he prays beautiful little prayers. The wonder of listening to children pray is that their prayers are so full of thankfulness. Whereas an adult's prayer is mostly made up of 'Please God, do You think You could . . . . ', followed by a shopping list of requests, children fill their prayers with thanks for all kinds of things that have made them happy — a sunny day, a trip to the beach, an ice-cream, mummy and daddy, and so on. Young children only seem to ask for things in their prayers if someone is sick, or something is lost, or there is another urgent need.

Bethany was quite tiny when her great-grandpa gave her a piece of his special chocolate. She popped it into her mouth, and I waited for the 'thank you'. It was a long time coming so I whispered, 'What do you say, darling?' and smiled encouragingly. She waited till she had finished enjoying every last, delicious, melting moment, then turned to Great-grandpa with a heart-stopping smile. 'More!' she said, with such enthusiasm he couldn't resist her request! Sometimes we're like that with God. He gives us a wonderful treat, and before we even say 'Thank You' we are asking for more and more.

I'm not saying we shouldn't ask God for things; He is just waiting for us to ask so He can pour the blessings down on us; but maybe we should spend more time thanking Him specifically for the myriad gifts He has already given us, most of which we take so easily for granted.

Dear Father, thank You for all those things you do for me which I will never realize until You share them with me in heaven. Amen.

Try some of these things today:

Make a list of lots of things for which you want to thank God. See if you can come up with at least fifty! It may be easier than you think! If so — try to find a hundred! Keep the list where you will see it often, or fold it into your Bible.

Write all the letters of the alphabet down the left-hand edge of a piece of paper. As a family, take it in turns to find different things for which you are thankful, with each item beginning with the next letter of the alphabet.

Each day, note in a diary the special things that you want to thank God for, as an individual, or as a family.

Write a thank you letter to God.

Help your children make a 'thank you' scrapbook, filled with pictures and other bits and pieces. Label each page, 'Thank you God for animals', or clothes, flowers, family, church, friends, holidays, etc.

Angel in his heart

It had been another one of those days. A disturbed night meant I'd woken late. Bernie had to go out early, and needed a packed lunch; the children wanted their breakfast, and then they had to be washed and dressed. You know, the usual things.

I had always intended to make sure that I looked nice and attractive, especially for my family, but it was even hard to find the time to brush my hair, let alone curl it or do anything else. If I did decide to curl it, I'd usually find myself sitting on the floor of the bedroom playing with a toddler, or reading a story at the same time.

A couple of pregnancies still hadn't completely shed themselves from my once slender body, and the practicalities of nursing babies meant I'd usually be wearing jog suits, and jeans, and not my favourite Laura Ashley dresses (presents from my mum!).

So, I felt saggy and baggy, frumpy and drab, before the day had barely begun. And by the evening I was also adorned with gluey fingerprints, globs of dried-on cereal, and grass stains from a frolic in the garden. Oh, yes, the baby had also been sick in my hair, and every now and then the fragrance of a cheese factory wafted past my face. I bathed the children, and dried them, one at a time, sitting on my lap. The inevitable happened, and while I caught most of the puddle in the towel, I could feel a warm wet area spreading down the leg of my jeans. Oh, well, I thought, I'll change and have a shower once they're all in bed. I rebathed the wet child, and powdered and dressed them all for bed. We had a story, and a prayer, and I was gratefully tucking them in for the night when a happy, cosy, drowsy little boy turned to me, and said, 'Mummy, you look just like an angel!'

I didn't feel like an angel, and I knew that I looked more like the prodigal son in the pigsty than anything celestial. But I smiled, and stored away those words in a special corner of my heart. One day, I hope and pray, Nathan will see a real angel in perfect beauty and loveliness. Here, he knows he has a guardian angel who is with him every minute of the day and night. It must be wonderful to look like an angel, so perfect, so beautiful, so spotless, but it's not looks that count when you are an angel. The important thing is being there for the one you care for, providing, protecting, loving . . .

I'm no angel, but I have also been with him every minute of the day, meeting his needs, protecting him and loving him, through everything that he's done, and it shows. It shows in my hair; it shows on my clothes; it shows in the tired lines, and the smiles on my face. But, most of all, I hope it shows in his heart.

Dear Father, thank You for the words of my little children that encourage me, and warm my heart. I pray that the little things I say to You may warm Your heart, too. And thank You for real angels. Amen.

Think of some treasured comments that your children have made, over the years, and write them out below.

Think of something special you can say to each member of your family today, to encourage them, and make them smile. Write down some ideas to help you.

Someone once said that the most beautiful thing in a child's world was his mother's face. How does this make you feel? Does this idea change the way you see yourself? . . . the way you see your child?

When the bough breaks . . .

Becoming a mother wasn't as easy as I'd thought. I suppose it never is. Our first pregnancy was a little unexpected, but we were soon delighted about the idea. I rushed out and bought a mother's journal to fill with all the romantic thoughts I would have as I drifted through the next few months, determined to wallow in the wonderful experience that was taking over my body. I read everything I could about pregnancy, took vitamins, went to bed early, and walked on cloud nine, all for about a week, and then the nausea set in, and none of my clothes would fit, and the three flights of stairs up to our apartment felt like Mount Everest!

I went for a check-up. The doctor seemed to be a bit concerned that he hadn't picked up a heartbeat with his super new machine, but I wasn't too worried. I thought that the heartbeat of a foetus was not detectable for several more months, so I didn't think about it much.

Then, one day at work, I began to spot blood. A little, then more and more. I didn't want to make a fuss, so I carried on, and called Bernie to collect me as I didn't feel up to driving thirty miles home on my own. By the end of the day I was feeling rather hazy.

That night we sat together, and didn't know what to say, or even what to expect. The duty doctor told me to 'keep everything solid', and take painkillers if it hurt. His advice did nothing to prepare us for the horror of that night.

We went to bed, and finally, at about 2am, I began to

have mini-contractions. I was bleeding copiously. Collecting everything solid proved to be a nightmare. I fainted, vomited, became almost delirious, and ended up in the Emergency Room where I was referred to as 'the lady having an abortion'.

I lay back on the trolley after everyone had left the room, and sobbed and sobbed. I felt such a failure. I wondered what was wrong with me, and why I hadn't been able to keep the baby. I hoped the lab tests would tell me something. A few days later the lab rang. All that we had managed to collect in a jar at home had been a large blood clot, and a piece of placenta. We had flushed the baby down the toilet. I was more devastated than ever.

I prayed; I tried to study to find some answers, but every time I talked to God all I could ask was 'Why?' I learned that it was OK to ask God 'Why?' It does not mean you doubt Him: it means that you trust Him with the most challenging questions in your life. After all, Jesus asked 'Why?' when He was on the cross.

I worked through the grief, in ups and downs, had another miscarriage six months later, and then, shortly after, conceived Bethany.

It's only been recently that some of my 'Why?' questions have been answered. I might have been a bit dense at the time, but six years later, when I was writing about my experiences for a book*, I began to ask God again why we had to lose the baby down the toilet. I heard the whisper, 'because it was for your best.' I still couldn't understand why it was so necessary, but the more I thought about it I realized that maybe there was something horribly wrong with its tiny form that would have troubled me more than its loss. I wondered why I'd had the miscarriage at all, and then realized that if I had had that baby, I would never have had Bethany, and she has given us so much happiness and love.

This side of heaven we don't know all the answers and

we never shall. My God is plenty big enough to handle my 'Why?'s. He doesn't want to see any of His children suffer, any more than we like to watch our own children have their jabs, or struggle with a fever, bump their knees, or have major surgery. He's watched His only Son suffer the greatest suffering in the universe, to put an end to our suffering. He's been through all the challenges of parenthood — a third of His angelic children rebelled; lied about His character; destroyed human lives, and dreamed up every agony on earth. Whatever comes our way we can know He's been there, and He cares. He holds us when we cry through the night. He feels every nuance of our pain. When everyone else has forgotten that the pain was ever there, He still remembers, and reaches out a comforting hand.

Becoming a parent isn't an easy task. A child that once brought the greatest joy, can one day bring you the greatest sadness, no matter how perfect your parenting skills. Being a parent challenges you to the very core of your being. It turns your life upside-down. It can exhilarate you, or drive you to despair. But, thank God, we are not alone, and, whatever happens, He always cares.

Dear Father, thank You that nothing, however traumatic, can ever separate me from Your love. Help me to turn to You when things get tough, and not away from You. You are the only One who can really understand, and really help. Thank You for always being there. Amen.

Think about the things that you would find hardest to cope with as a parent. List them, and then imagine the list belongs to God, and it details all the things He has already experienced.

Thank Him that He can truly understand all we may ever have to suffer, and more. Then let yourself be filled with confidence for the future as you and God face it together, in His infinite love and wisdom.

Pray for all the parents you know who are hurting, or discouraged.

Make contact with a friend who has had a miscarriage, or other painful experience, and do something special together. Let her feel free to share anything that is on her heart, and listen to what she says without judgement or criticism, just pure acceptance.

If you have been through a challenging experience, maybe you can find time to share what's on your heart with an understanding friend, or write a letter to God, telling Him all about your feelings.

* 'The Loneliest Grief', Karen Holford, Autumn House Publishing, 1994.

When you get to the end of your rope . . .

The phone rang, and a friend called. She was feeling low, and unable to cope; could she come and spend a couple of days with us? 'Yes! Of course! We'd love to see you!' I heard my voice say. After a few more minutes of chatter I put down the telephone and slumped into a chair. I was exhausted! I felt I had nothing left to give that would be of any help to my friend, who was going through a marital breakdown. We had a new baby, I was still recovering from flu, we were trying to plan a major seminar for the following week, and our church was going through a severe crisis. I wanted to go somewhere quiet and bury my head in the sand. To be honest, the last thing I needed was to spend two days in intense counselling with my friend. I needed someone to give me a bit of a lift, too.

'Dear Father, help me. I feel drained of any energy to cope with Susi. I don't know how I can be of any use to her. I have barely enough strength left to cope with my own life right now. If you are sending her to us for a purpose, then please fill up my reserve tank, so I can make it through the next few days. Thank You. Amen.' I picked up my Bible to try and find something in it that would give me a few more inches of rope to cling to before I reached the end of my tether.

I found this story. A familiar story. But now it had a fresh meaning as I sat at the kitchen table, with my tank running on 'empty'.

Once there were two people who were at the end of

their ropes. There was Elijah, sitting, hungry and parched, by the dried up brook . . . at the end of his resources . . . at the end of his road. And there was a widow . . . at the end of her flour . . . at the end of her oil . . . at the end of her hope.

By themselves they could do nothing. Each looked doomed to die. Both must have glimpsed more than a little despair, and wondered what God could possibly do to save the situation.

Apart, their lives seemed hopeless. But God brought them both together, there, outside the village of Zarephath. Elijah was almost fainting from fatigue and hunger; the widow may have been weeping as she collected the twigs together to fuel her last meal. God brought them together, and gave them hope. Even though they may have reached rock bottom from an earthly perspective, they still clung to their faith in God.

Elijah needed faith to leave the safe haven of the brook. The widow needed faith to believe that if she fed this strange man first, there would still be food for her own family. And through their faith they were preserved. But they also needed each other. God provided for them both in a way which made them interdependent on each other, as the flour and oil continued to flow from the widow's earthenware jars till the famine finally ended.

Susi came. 'I don't want to talk about anything right now; I just need to get away and have a bit of a break. Why don't we go shopping? I'll cook the dinner; you've got your hands full with the children. And when they're asleep, maybe you could show me how to do some stencilling . . . .' We talked and chatted, laughed and had fun together. She played with the children, and gave me time to rest, too. 'I'm so glad I came here,' she said when it was time to go. 'I always feel refreshed after I've been with you and the children. I feel I have much more energy now to take home with me, and maybe I can start again with John.'

Sometimes we come to the end of our ropes, our brooks, our oil jars. We may feel, as the widow might have done, that the last thing we need is another mouth to feed. Or we may feel like Elijah, and not want to leave the comfort of the brook, and face the dangers of the world again.

Famines may touch our lives. Emotional famines. Spiritual famines. Just at the times when we feel we have nothing left to give, God may bring us into contact with another 'starving' person. Our natural instinct may be to withdraw, to preserve whatever we have left for our own use. But even in our times of famine, God can use us to be a channel of His blessings to others. Our own weakness and lack of personal resources can mean that we are more open to being used by God to help others in need. And He will not let us down. He will make sure that there is always just enough oil and flour in our storage jars until the famine in our lives has passed once more.

Dear Father, when I feel weakest, help me to remember to turn to You for strength. When I don't feel strong, You are more able to channel Your great power through me, and I know it's You who are doing the wonderful things, and not I. Thank You for the times of weakness, because they let me feel more of Your power, and help me to depend on Your strength always, even when I naïvely feel I can cope on my own. Amen.

Can you think of any times when God has used you, in spite of your apparent weakness, or maybe even because of your weakness?

We all face many challenging moments when we feel vulnerable and exhausted. What do you do to help yourself cope in times like these? Make a list of things that you can do that will help to pick you up when things get tough.

Make a Promise List of texts that you find particularly encouraging. Collect them as you find them, and keep them handy so you can memorize them. Copy the list to share with someone else. You will find a list of texts at the end of this book, containing many special promises for you.

Of slugs, snails and butterflies' tales

Nathan loves to collect 'creepy-crawlies'. Caterpillars are the most exciting for him. He collects them and feeds them on leaves until they turn into chrysalises. Together we watched a red admiral butterfly emerge from its dull-looking cocoon, its blood pumping through to the tips of its new wings. We put the butterfly on a sunny flower to dry out, and then saw it suddenly flutter and dance through the summer sky, elated by a taste of freedom after days of cramped confinement.

Nathan has such a love for God's little creatures that we even have to be kind to the slugs and snails in our garden! We collect up all the snails he finds, and keep them in a special container, until we can go out to the lanes nearby, and let them go in a safe place, away from humans and prize chrysanthemums. Once, when he was 2, he found a dead slug, and made a nest for it in an old plastic container. We tried to tell him it was dead, but he wouldn't believe us. 'No,' he said, 'it's only asleep; I'm sure I saw it move.' After a couple of days we had to bury it.

One day I entered the kitchen to find a particularly ugly specimen of a snail on the worktop. It was large, muddy, and coated in cobwebs. I had to look at it hard for a while to work out what it was, but I knew immediately how it had arrived there. 'Nathan!' I called. It was one thing having to run an emigration service for snails, but they definitely weren't welcome in my home! Nathan came running. 'What's the matter, Mummy?' he said. 'This is the matter,' I said, pointing at the offending beast. 'What is it doing in the kitchen?' 'It's my pet!' Nathan was finding it difficult to appreciate my distaste for his latest acquisition. 'But why do we have to keep this snail?' I demanded. His next statement was a memorable one. 'Because it might turn into a butterfly, of course!'

It can be so easy to write people off because they don't seem to be able to offer anything positive. Maybe they look ugly, and dirty. Maybe their habits aren't too pleasant. Maybe we just don't know how to get along with them. We decide we don't want them in our homes, but we try to do what we can for them, in the same way that we helped the snails emigrate. We may offer them help-programmes, or soup-kitchens, or even a dutiful smile as we pass by. But do we see them as Jesus sees them? Jesus specialized in collecting friends that no one else wanted. He saw their potential. He knew that every slug, snail, spider or worm could turn into a beautiful butterfly. He had that much faith; that much love, for each one of His creatures, whoever they were. Do we?

Dear Father, help me to see people as You see them. Help me to see beyond the grubby, ugly exteriors, and see the beautiful potential of butterflies within. Please help me to love them. Amen.

How can you help some of the snails in your world turn into butterflies?

List some of the potential attributes and skills your children may have. Begin encouraging them now. Help them to develop these positive characteristics and practise their talents.

When you talk to your children, try focusing on their 'butterfly wings', rather than nagging them about their 'dusty shells', and watch them emerge from their cocoons with brighter colours.

God's timing — no accident!

For the first time in years I was beginning to feel in control of my life. Our new home felt like a palace. Nathan was finally potty-trained. At last I was able to return to work as an occupational therapist for one day a week. My first book was almost completed. Everything in my life seemed to be coming together perfectly. I felt exhilarated and free. After five years of intense mothering, my life and body were just starting to feel like mine again! I felt full of inexpressible joy and peace, somehow like the sensation of rolling down a grassy slope on a warm summer day. My heart seemed to be singing to God all the time. I hadn't felt so wonderful in years! Not that I didn't enjoy babies, night feeds and nappies, but it was wonderful to feel that now I could have more time and energy to be with my children, and do exciting things with them. We were planning to home school for a couple of years, and I was looking forward to sharing the fun of finding out together.

The incredible sensation of blissful freedom lasted about a week. Still, it was good while it lasted. But then I started to feel a bit strange; sort of tired and sicky, and I started to buy grapefruit again. No, I can't believe this, I thought. We had been as careful as we could be. But we'd always joked about having 'two children and an accident'. A couple of days before realizing I was pregnant, we'd had a house-warming party, and almost the whole church had been there. One lady asked me if we were planning to have any more children, and I'd said a very firm 'No!' Soon they would all know I was pregnant again, and they'd know it was an 'accident'. I felt so humiliated. At first I didn't want to tell anyone, not even my Mum!

I was in a stunned state of shock for several weeks. I didn't mind another baby so much, but the thought of another pregnancy was enough to send me crazy. I am nauseous, and vomit frequently, for the entire nine months. All those romantic notions of glowing and being rosy, and enjoying the incredible experience dissolved rapidly, even before I unwrapped the pregnancy testing kit! Each pregnancy is even worse than the one before. Nothing takes away the horrible feeling of sickness except sleep, and, eventually, delivery!

One thing I was sure about, I never wanted to feel that a baby of ours was in any way 'unwanted', or even an 'accident'. I was sure that as far as God was concerned, my baby was no 'accident'. We had gone to such lengths trying not to conceive that God must have performed a miracle to achieve this conception!

But there were so many things I'd wanted to do! I'd been longing for a time when I could write more freely, work on a parenting seminar with Bernie, sew a quilt, create a flower garden, travel without buggies, high-chairs, cots and nappies, and wear dresses that didn't have front openings for discreet feeds. I'd been six years 'breeding and feeding' as Bernie once stated so succinctly, and I felt I deserved a rest. But now, another baby, another three or four years of intense mothering, caring and watching. It would sap me of time and energy to spend doing all the great things I wanted to do with Bethany and Nathan. I was fighting depression for weeks. I felt guilty because we had so many friends who were having problems having babies, and my problem was that I couldn't seem to *stop* having them!

One thing I learnt, as the depression began to lift, was that God's timing was different to mine. Another three years or so of pregnancy and babyhood seemed like an eternity to me. But then I stood back from my life, and began to look at it God's way, and the way I would look at it myself, one day. Nine years of babying, out of a lifetime, didn't seem that much. One day I will look back on my life from an ancient rocking chair, and remember the baby years with great fondness, and yearn for them once more. Maybe I will even wish they'd lasted longer than nine years, which isn't so long out of seventy, is it? The book, the back-opening dresses, and the quilt would just have to wait a few years. I'd always found God's timing to be perfect, in retrospect, so I would be able to trust His perfect timing for this baby, too . . .

Now, a couple of years later, I think God helped me write this book *because* I had a baby, rather than *in spite* of having a baby! I realize that most of the manuscript has been written while I've been sitting up in bed, feeding Joel. Maybe, just maybe, if I hadn't had him, this book might still be only a few ideas scratched on the back of a shopping list . . . !

Dear Father, thank You that You know the end from the beginning, and that Your perfect timing in my life can surprise me with Your perfect joy. Amen.

List all the joys you have had, and dreams that have been fulfilled *because* you had children, rather than *in spite* of having them.

Think of a time when God's timing was perfect, although it might not have been a part of your original plan.

Spend a few moments praising God for His timing, even in those circumstances where you are still unsure about His plans for you.

Heavenly motherhood

As soon as I found out that we were expecting our third child, I decided to let 5-year-old Bethany in on the secret. I was always very sick when I was pregnant, and we thought the children would be less worried for me if they knew that I was being sick for a special reason. But I didn't want to excite them too much. Because of the two miscarriages I'd had before Bethany and Nathan were born, I knew that pregnancy held many hazards.

'Bethany,' I said, 'We have something special to tell you. Mummy is pregnant, and there is a little baby growing inside her, which is why she is being so sick.'

'Mummy, I'm so pleased! I was praying you'd have another baby!'

'But, Bethany, I just want you to know that not all babies work out. Some of them die before they are born. It's very sad. We hope and pray this baby will be all right, but we'll have to wait and see.'

'Never mind, Mummy,' she said. 'If your baby dies, then you'll be able to have a little baby in heaven when you get there. Won't that be nice?' We'd never talked about such things, but somehow children have a fresh way of understanding God that most adults seem to have lost over the years.

In an old book I once read a portrayal of the second coming of Jesus. It had a beautiful description of angels reuniting babies and their mothers at the resurrection, but my thoughts had never progressed much past that point. Now I found myself imagining being a mother in heaven. What bliss! But I could hardly envisage rows of pearly-white nappies hanging on a celestial washing line outside a golden mansion! The heavenly babies in my imagination didn't need nappy changes! It would be wonderful to be a mother with boundless energy and minimal housework. There would be no teething pain, no croup and fevers to struggle with at midnight, no days feeling heavy-headed from lack of sleep, no temper tantrums, no teenage terrors, no fear of dangers . . . . Just the joy of being together in a perfect world, sharing the delights of paradise, watching the child grow to its fullest potential, naturally and perfectly. Motherhood as it was meant to be.

We don't know all that heaven has to offer. My wildest imaginings probably seem completely inadequate compared to the reality that God has prepared for us. But I do know that God is making it a place where all our sadnesses will end, and pure, eternal happiness will begin. God's love is preparing an eternity of unimaginable joys for each one of us, whatever our earthly sorrows have been.

Dear Father, thank You for preparing a heaven for us that will be beyond anything we can dream or imagine. Help me to create a little piece of heaven on earth in our home, and help me prepare my family for a future together eternally. Amen.

What is it about heaven that you look forward to most of all?

Spend time with your children talking about the things they want to do in heaven. Let the younger ones draw a picture of the whole family in heaven, doing special things.

What can you do to make heaven start right now, in your own home?

Sticky tape and nails

It was Easter time, and for family worship we were building a model of Calvary out of Lego bricks. We stacked them up to make a hill; made three crosses to put on the top, and even constructed a cave in the side of the hill for the tomb. We found a tiny Lego person, and adjusted the design of the cross and the tomb, so that we could fix 'Jesus' onto the cross, and then fit him into the tomb.

Bethany and Nathan told the story about Jesus' being put on the cross, and then being laid in the tomb. They made a Lego boulder to cover the entrance of the tomb, and found some Lego soldiers to guard it. When we read the story of the resurrection, the Lego boulder was taken away; the soldiers fell over, and 'Jesus' was taken out of the tomb. Then we all sang a praise song.

After worship, Bethany was trying to put 'Jesus' back on the cross. It was tricky for her little fingers. The cross was fragile, and kept breaking under the pressure. It was difficult to move the Lego figure's arms so that he could be fixed to the 'cross' bricks. Finally she gave up, and asked me to do it for her. As I reassembled all the little bits Bethany asked, 'How did they fix Jesus on the cross to make Him die?'

'Well, the Roman soldiers hammered nails through His hands, and into the wood of the cross.'

'Oh, that's horrible! It must have hurt a lot! Is that why He died?'

'It wasn't just the hurt hands. Being on a cross makes

it hard to breathe, and Jesus was sad, and hurt a lot inside, too, because He was dying for everyone's sins.'

Bethany thought about all of this in the way little children think about things that are difficult to fit into their own experience and understanding. Then she picked up the Lego cross. By this time 'Jesus' was fixed back onto it. She slowly turned the figure in her hands.

'I expect they only used nails to fix Him on because they didn't have any sticky tape in those days.' She stood the little cross back on the black brick hill.

Children have a wonderful way of believing the best in other people, and expecting the best, as well. It's often hard for them to understand how people can be cruel and evil to one another. Occasionally Bethany will hear a snippet of news — a bomb attack that killed the father of four in Northern Ireland — children shot and killed in Sarajevo while playing with their sledges in the snow — a child murdered by two young boys, and you can see from her face that she finds it hard to believe that people can be so terrible.

It is a simple, trusting innocence that helps a child believe the best about the world. As we grow older we are hurt, our trust is broken, and even before we are adults, we may have become cynical, and quick to jump to negative conclusions about people's behaviour.

Psychologists have discovered that children tend to become what we believe about them. If we believe the best about a child, he or she will do much better than if we believe the worst. People who believe the best about us encourage us and spur us on to do greater things. One of my editors writes me a positive letter every time he needs a new article, or if he thinks I haven't written for a while. Whenever I hear from him it makes me want to write more; he believes I can do it, and I don't want to let him down. I keep all his letters to read in those dark moments when I am stricken by writer's block! My editor understands about the need to believe the best in others if you want to get the best out of them.

Jesus believes the best about us. He believed it was worth dying for you, personally. He loves you that much. He knows that there are others out there who want to think only the worst about you, and bring you down, but He wanted to show you that He could leave heaven and die for you, and lift you up forever, above all the negativity and suspicion in the world.

Dear Father, thank You for believing the best about each one of us. Help me to look for the best in each person I meet today, and help me to find ways to let them know they are special to me, as well as to You. Amen.

Write out the names of all the members in your family, and under each name list ten positive things about each person.

Then let each one know, with a little note, or a quiet, cosy chat and a hug, just how much you appreciate them.

Do you believe the best about Jesus? Or are you limiting Him by your own lack of faith?

Another nine months of nausea?!

I'd always had a romantic notion of what it was like to be pregnant. I think I had a sort of vision of myself, glowing with health and happiness, contemplating the little life within, while sitting in a rocking chair sewing pastel quilts. For years I had looked forward to the time when I would cook Bernie a candlelit supper, then gaze deep into his eyes and tell him he was going to become a father.

The reality was somewhat more down-to-earth. No secret trips to the doctor, no romantic evening to break the news. Even before I was a few days 'late' I was rushing to the bathroom almost every hour of the day. I was so sick I couldn't even read for weeks! I could barely face opening the kitchen door, let alone standing there and cooking; and a romantic supper? the way I felt? you've got to be joking! As soon as I was aware that I was pregnant, Bernie knew too. I would turn green, vomit at even the thought of food, and sleep thirteen hours a day — more if I could get it. Morning sickness lasted all day for nine months of sheer misery. Each pregnancy made me even sicker than before. I was so ill that I could easily have prayed for a miscarriage to put an end to the horrible feelings in my body that nothing would relieve. And that was after having already lost two pregnancies, and being desperate for a baby.

When I was pregnant with Bethany it was miserable, but I didn't have to care for anyone else, except Bernie, and he could cope on his own if necessary. When

Bethany was 2, I was pregnant with Nathan, and she learned how to fetch me glasses of water from the bathroom. Daddy was out pastoring in the evenings, and I needed to sleep longer hours than Bethany, so I would shut the bedroom door, and I would sleep next to her, while she sat and looked at a pile of books. Finally she would fall asleep, and Daddy would carry her to her bed when he came home.

Nathan had just been potty-trained when I was pregnant with Joel. I was so ill I couldn't even help him in the bathroom. He would call and call for me, and I knew I couldn't move without being sick. Bethany would have to go and help him with his clothes, and wash his little hands.

Each time I was pregnant I prayed and prayed that the awful nausea would go away. It seemed all wrong to me that I should feel so sick when it was more important than ever to have a healthy diet, and be fit and strong. The horrible feelings almost drove me crazy. I would sleep just to get away from the nausea. Someone once described how it felt to undergo chemotherapy, and it sounded just like my pregnancies, except my hair didn't fall out.

When I found out that I was pregnant for the third time, I groaned. 'No, God,' I said, 'please, not another nine months of physical torture! Why me? Why don't You choose one of my many friends who say they never feel better than when they're pregnant? Or someone who has been waiting years to conceive? Why me, again? I don't think I can bear that dreadful feeling another time . . . . Well, if You do want me to have another baby — please could You make it feel nice this time, and take away all this yuckiness! Please let me have *one* enjoyable pregnancy in my life!'

The sickness didn't go away. This time it was worse than ever before. I complained to Bernie. Bernie is very good for me. He is so calm. As one of our friends puts it,

'He is so "laid back" — he's horizontal!' He has to be that way to cope with me. We need someone logical and unflappable in our relationship to compensate for my wild emotional and 'artistic' temperament. He's almost all Phlegmatic, and I'm a Melancholic temperament — I bring beauty and order to his life, and he brings rationality and calmness into mine. He also comes in extra handy when I have a deep theological question like this: 'I'm fed up with being sick! It's horrible! I can't stand this feeling in my body a minute longer! Why doesn't God take it away? Why doesn't He heal me? What is the point of this senseless nausea and vomiting? It's not doing anyone a bit of good, especially the baby!' I flung the words around angrily and bitterly. Then I paused for breath — too much yelling and I'd be off to the bathroom again.

'You know,' he said calmly, after a minute or two, 'if you weren't so sick, God would have a hard time keeping you still enough to have a baby!' I was stunned into silence by his response. I'd never quite looked at it that way before. I paused, and reflected. Maybe he was right. I even smiled. Who was I, a mere mortal, to question God? What was nine months of nausea in a lifetime, or eternity? And every minute of that misery was certainly a small price to pay for the gift of a child's life.

Dear Father, Thank You that Jesus was willing to suffer so that I could be Your child for eternity. Please strengthen me when I face suffering and challenges of many different kinds, and as I try to guide my children towards eternity. Thank You for the beautiful things that can come out of my suffering. Help me to find those things, and focus on them, when sometimes the suffering seems more than I can bear. Amen.

What are some of the special challenges and difficulties you have had, or are still facing in your life?

List your challenges, and then try to write at least one positive thing that has arisen from each of them.

Any suffering is worth it for the gift of a child's life — our children are very precious. Find a way today to tell them how precious they are to you. Maybe you could slip a note into their lunch boxes, or under their pillows.

In the secret place

One of the most delightful things about being pregnant for the third time was that at last we lived in a place where it was possible to have a 'photo' of our baby's ultra-sound scan. When I was pregnant with Bethany, I was desperate to have a picture of the scan, but the hospital didn't have the facilities to provide one. After my miscarriages I needed extra reassurance that the baby was really there, and that everything was all right. When I was scanned for Nathan at another hospital, there were no photos either, so I was thrilled to be able to have a scan-photo of our third baby.

We all went into the ultra-sound room together, and the children watched the baby on the monitor. The technician showed them the baby's hands, and they counted all the fingers and toes. They saw the heart beating, and the bladder emptying. They saw the baby's face, and its little arm seemed to wave at them. The new baby sibling was becoming a reality in their lives too. I kept the scan-photo in my diary, looking at it in quiet, secret moments, imagining the baby within my body, loving its little turned-up nose and miniature features.

But really, I don't need a photo. I fall in love with my babies the minute I know they are a reality, tucked deep within the tiny folds of my being, growing secretly and silently. It seems funny to be in love with someone I have never seen or touched or heard, and someone whose presence makes me feel so utterly dreadful! But when that baby is flesh of my flesh, and life of my life, I just can't help it. I am bound to our child from the minute of its conception.

Dear Baby,

Even though you have no name, I love you. You are my life, and without my life, you could not be. I can feel you move, but I cannot touch you. I've watched you move, but I've never seen you. I cannot hold you close and comfort you, even though you are closer to me than any other human being. And yet you are so far away, because you are just out of reach.

My arms ache to hold you, but one day they will ache from holding you. I know this is crazy, but I long to take you out, hold you close, and caress you. I want to whisper how much I love you, and drink in all that you are, and then to put you back again, for safe-keeping, until birth.

It won't be long now. Soon we shall find each other, and touch and gaze, and learn to know each other. I will wrap you in my arms and hold you tight. We shall be separated, but, no matter what happens, we shall always be a part of each other.

I love you,
Mummy.

Dear Child,

I know you by name, and I love you so much I gave My life for you. Without My life, you could not live. I have watched your every move, even before you were born. Because I can live in you, I can be closer to you than any human being, even though you cannot see Me or touch Me directly. But you know I am there, because you can feel Me in other ways, and listen to Me whispering in your heart.

My arms ache to hold you. I wish I could take you out of the world, right now, and keep you here safely in heaven, protected and comforted. But we must be patient, and wait awhile.

It won't be long now. Soon we shall be together for eternity. You will see Me, and touch Me. We shall share a wonderful hug. And nothing in the whole universe will ever separate us again.

I love you.

Your ever-loving Father,

God.

'Though you have not seen him, you love him; and even though you do not see him now, you believe in him and are filled with an inexpressible and glorious joy. 1 Peter 1:8.

Dear Father, thank You for letting me share in this wonderful experience of creating new life. I am looking forward to being with You, in person, forever. I love You, too. Amen.

Think about some of the special things you thought about your unborn child when you were pregnant.

Describe how it felt to be a part of God's creative pattern, as a new life grew within you.

Write a letter to God, telling Him how much you want Him to be a part of your life.

Desperate for delivery!

I lay in bed. It was early evening, but I was thirty-eight weeks pregnant, and I'd had a tiring day. I was fed up. I ached all over, and was uncomfortable whatever I did. I was hugely pregnant and still being sick. Boy, was I miserable!

I lay in the dark and talked to God. 'Dear Father, please can You do something! I've had thirty-eight weeks of utter misery with this pregnancy. I always have big babies — this one must be quite a size by now. It's all fully grown, and another two weeks won't make much difference. I certainly don't need another two weeks of this — I'll just get even fatter, and even more tired, and cross with the children. It's my birthday next week, and it would be so good to have delivered by then . . . . Please, Father, do something soon!'

Afterwards I felt a bit ashamed of myself. I wondered whether it was right to talk to God like that. Was it irreverent and presumptuous? I didn't really know. Bernie was busy, so I couldn't ask him about it. I drifted off into a welcome sleep, still feeling slightly guilty.

Bernie came to bed at one o'clock in the morning. He didn't usually stay up that late, but he had some extra preparation to do for the church service in the morning. I woke then, and we chatted a bit, until he stopped answering me, and I knew he'd gone to sleep at last.

The house was quiet. I wasn't really sleepy any more; I'd already slept five hours. I lay, and thought about all kinds of things, and what we ought to call the baby.

Slowly I realized that I was having very mild contractions. I'd had lots of them during this pregnancy, and so I didn't take much notice. I began to time them by the illuminated clock on the bedroom shelf. Yes, they were about every five minutes. I poked Bernie. He was deep asleep. 'Bernie, I think you ought to know I'm having lots of contractions!' He groaned and rolled over. He hadn't heard. I poked him again, and spoke a bit louder.

'Ughhh,' he grunted. 'Just wake me up if you need me.' Poor thing, he was really exhausted. My parents weren't planning to come to help me until the next day. The children were sleeping; we'd have to take them to the hospital with us — no one we knew would take them at this hour in the night! My case was packed — I just needed snacks for Bernie and the children, and their sleeping bags. I was beginning to get excited. One of the positive things about having such rotten pregnancies is that I look forward to labour with utter delight! The end is at last nigh! Soon I'll have my baby, and I'll stop being sick!

I nudged Bernie again. 'I think you need to wake up, darling.' I got up and walked around, slightly stunned, trying to think about what I needed to do before I left home, hoping upon hope that this wasn't a false alarm. I quickly showered and did my hair — just in case Bernie wanted to take any photos, then went back to try to wake him properly.

It was a crazy day. My parents had to drive down a day earlier than expected to collect the children waiting with us in the delivery room. Bernie had to find someone else to preach in his place that morning, with two hours' notice. The children were happy to be with me — Bethany had wanted to see the birth anyway! — but fortunately my labour slowed down until Grandma and Grandpa arrived to whisk them off home again.

At last there was just Bernie and I in the delivery room. 'I wonder what made you go into labour two weeks early,' said Bernie. 'You've always been on time before.'

'Do you really want to know?' I asked with a smile on my face. 'I had a good talk to God about things last night, and I suggested that another two weeks being pregnant wasn't really necessary. I guess He agreed with me!'

'You did what?!' Bernie was incredulous. 'You could have waited another day — then your parents would have been here, and I could still have taken the service . . . !'

Maybe I should have waited. I don't know. But I do know that my God listens, and He cares for me, and above all He knows just how much I can take! Mentally, I threw my arms around His loving body and gave Him the biggest hug I could!

Dear Father, thank You that I can come to You with all my needs, whatever they are, and ask You for help. Thank You that You listen, and care for me, and that You remember that I am as fragile as dust. Amen.

Think about a time when God has answered your prayers in a special way.

Has God ever given you relief in a miraculous way, just when you felt you couldn't take any more? Write about it.

Do our prayers change God's plans; or does the Spirit guide us to pray for the right things at the right time, so that we will be encouraged and strengthened when our requests are granted? What do you think is happening when we pray?

What do you especially need to ask God for today? Pray about it.

Tomorrow is another day

It had been one of those days. One of those days when everything I touched seemed to fall apart, drop on the floor, make a mess or draw blood. I was having one mini disaster after another. I'd had only about six hours' sleep, caring for baby Joel, who was barely eight weeks old. He was having a fussy day, and he cried whenever he wasn't being held, so I was carrying him about, and my arms ached from the weight. Bethany and Nathan were being argumentative, and, no matter what they did, they ended up in a fight. They ignored my requests; hated my food, and flooded the bathroom. When I finally lulled Joel off to sleep, they had another fight and woke him up. I seemed to spend all day asking them to do things they wouldn't do, until I got more and more frustrated and began to yell. I felt dreadful. It seemed I was being totally ineffective. I couldn't discipline them, and nothing seemed to make any of them happy. I tried to plan something fun for us to do together when Joel was asleep. Finally he dropped off again, and I sorted out all the bits we needed. He slept for five minutes, then woke up, and I had to feed him again. Meanwhile, Bethany and Nathan got into everything and messed up all the pieces, and it took me another hour to clear up all the chaos.

Exhausted, I was relieved when it was time for them to go to bed. But once again they played up, larking around, and disobeying. I told Nathan off for not putting his pyjamas on, and he burst into tears, dived into his bed, and cried, 'I want my Daddy! My Mummy doesn't love me any more!' I dived into my bed and cried too. I thought what a lousy, rotten mother I was. I was useless. They didn't like my food. They didn't obey me. I couldn't even do fun things with them any more, because I had to care for Joel so much. I had wanted to be a stay-at-home Mum, and be there for them always, and do wonderful things with them, but it never worked out. I was always so busy, always so tired. Maybe they'd be better off without me . . . .

Funny, earlier in the week Bernie and I had been discussing one of our friends. She had left her two young sons with her husband and gone off to make a new life for herself, not even getting in touch with her children. 'How could she do such a thing?' we wondered. 'How could a mother leave her children, after such intense nurturing?' I couldn't bear to be apart from my children for more than a few hours!

But that was earlier in the week, and this was now. And now I felt like a failed mother. I felt sure no one else could ever be as bad at mothering as I had been. No, I knew I couldn't leave them. I loved them so much it hurt. And it hurt to feel that my love wasn't able to get through to them, because there was so much frustration and fatigue in the way. They could really do without me nagging and yelling all the time. Maybe that was why our friend had left her children? . . . .

I lay in bed after they were all asleep and prayed. 'Father, I feel such a useless mother. Today everything seemed to go wrong. Even when I tried to do special things with the children, it ended in disaster. I seemed to spend a whole day being cross with them. Why does my discipline seem so ineffective? What am I doing wrong? How long can I carry on like this? Why did You give us another child when I could barely cope with the first two?' My thoughts grew more and more desperate. I just piled them all into my prayer and dumped them at

God's feet. I went on and on, rehearsing all my failures, detailing all my difficulties.

Finally, I was too exhausted to say any more. I lay in the darkness, desperate and depressed, waiting for Bernie to come home from his evening meeting. The house was quiet. My storm was over, and, in the subdued silence, I heard a still small voice inside my heart. It said, simply, reassuringly, 'Just go to sleep; it won't be so bad in the morning.' The words echoed through my mind as I drifted peacefully off into my dreams.

The next day the children were like little angels. They were so good and obedient. Bethany wanted to help wherever she could. There were no fights. Joel slept well. We all had fun together. I finished the housework quickly, and the children managed to eat a meal without once using the word 'Yucky!'

Dear Father, You were right! It wasn't so bad in the morning! Thank You for new beginnings, and refreshing sleep! Amen.

Can you think of a day that seemed utterly disastrous? How do you feel about it now? Can you laugh about it? Can you even draw a cartoon about it? Some experiences are no laughing matter, but how can you begin to feel peace in the situation?

If you have been facing some challenging times, make today a new beginning. Put aside the feelings and experiences that were part of yesterday, and let them go. Forget the failures and tell yourself that you are the best mother your children could ever have. Have a fresh start today.

Whenever you come into moments of conflict or stress, pause a moment and pray for help. Then take a deep breath, smile, and see if it makes a difference.

'I want to be just like you, Mummy!'

It's quite flattering, really, when Bethany wants to look like me. She likes it when we can dress the same way, and when I let her use some of the flowery perfume that Bernie bought me for our wedding anniversary. If you ask her what she would like to be when she grows up, she says she wants to do what Mummy does. When someone once asked her what that was, she said she would be an occupational therapist on Mondays, a writer on Tuesdays, a Mummy on Wednesdays, a crafts-person on Thursdays, and a Pastor's wife on Fridays! Actually, my life is not as neatly organized as that! Usually all the jobs get bundled together and spread throughout the week!

There are other ways in which Bethany is like me. For one, she likes to read, just as I did, all the time. It's great to see how much she reads, and it's fun to share my old, favourite books with her. But, just like me, she can't resist reading after bedtime: 'Just to the end of the chapter, Mummy, I promise.' And the chapter lasts almost an hour! I remember trying to read that last, crucial chapter by the light of the street lamp outside my bedroom window. She also likes to dream up new designs for things, and make little presents for other people, just as I do. As a child I hated peas, potatoes, tomatoes and milk; those are exactly the same things that Bethany doesn't like to eat. It seems she inherited my tastebuds, too.

The other day I chided one of the children for picking

up the steamed broccoli with his fingers and popping it into his mouth without using a fork. 'But that's the way you do it, Mummy!' a little voice protested. And I realized that several years of trying to feed a little one, cutting vegetables for the older ones, feeding myself, and chatting to Bernie, were seriously eroding my table manners!

Another day I was encouraging the children to tidy their rooms, as they both had friends coming to stay. Nathan finished his room, and then popped his head around our bedroom door. Bernie's clothes were scattered by his bedside; heaps of papers lay strewn on my desk, and the laundry basket was overflowing. 'Oh, dear!' said Nathan, 'I don't think I can let you have your pocket money this week until you've done something about this mess!'

One of the first things all of our children learned to say was 'Oh, dear!' because I seemed to say it every few minutes as I rushed from one calamity to the next!

We feel so proud when our children emulate our best bits, and when they like doing the things that we also enjoy. But it can be embarrassing, humiliating and frustrating when they pick up our less desirable traits! Our children have each acquired a few of these from us, but I'm not going to tell you what they are! Some of them are almost unprintable!

But it's when I see my own negative traits displayed before me in the mirror of my children that I feel more motivated to change! I'm aware of quite a few of my 'defects', but I hope that most of them don't show! My children are around me more than anyone else, 'beholding' me all day and every day. They see me at my worst, and at my best. I want to be more like God. I want to be a good example for my children, and guide them into beautiful characters. But I know that it's only by my spending more time with God, and discovering His beautiful character, that He can give me the power to change.

And one day, one wonderful day, we will all be changed 'in the twinkling of an eye', 1 Corinthians 15:52.

Dear Father, help me to keep my eyes on You so that I will become more like You every day. Thank You. Amen.

In what ways are your children like you? What things have they inherited from you, and what have they picked up from watching you? How does this make you feel?

Choose one of your 'defects' or habits that you would like to eradicate. Talk to God about it: admit the problem; thank Him for helping you overcome it, and work on it together.

Read Psalm 103 and list all the characteristics of God you can find there. Spend some time thinking about the picture of God painted by this Psalm, and then spend a while 'beholding' Him.

A moment on the stairs

I have just been folding laundry, and stacking it in the different bedrooms. Soon I shall try to squeeze the piles into the wardrobes, drawers and cupboards, and onto the shelves. I have a big pile of laundry to carry up the stairs, so I decide to leave baby Jojo, as we call him, at the bottom. Trying to carry him and the laundry creates lots of ironing, and it can be a dangerous ride, so it's easier just to leave him in the hall, even if he does start to cry.

Bethany is horrified at the occasional times I have to leave Jojo crying. 'You never left me to cry when I was a baby . . . did you?!' She thinks I'm being heartless. She can't believe the Mummy she knows would ever leave her to cry. I'm glad she has that much faith in me, but as she watches Jojo cry, while I 'mercilessly' sort laundry, she obviously begins to wonder about my maternal instincts. One day she'll understand. I hope.

The job takes a few minutes, and then I return to the top of the stairs and look down. Joel is sitting at the bottom of the stairs crying as if his world has fallen apart. He has just learnt to crawl, but he hasn't worked out how to climb the stairs. The stair-gate is already in position, just in case he gets exploratory tendencies.

For a moment, I pause. I look down at the little red, screaming face. Jojo howls, but his eyes open wide when he sees me at the top of the stairs. He looks up at me beseechingly. All he wants is to be near me. But he is cut off and isolated by the gate, and his own physical immaturity. I could stand at the top and ask him to come to me. I could smile, and stretch out my arms for him, but it would be no good. It wouldn't bring him any closer, no matter how lovingly I responded to his cries.

He wants to be near me, and I want to be with him, too. But there is only one way. I walk down the stairs, open the gate, and gather his sobbing little body against my chest. I hug him till he stops crying, and then he grins and grins, because he knows he's achieved exactly what he wanted.

The whole episode lasts only a few moments, but as I walk down the stairs I suddenly see myself as a tiny child, constrained by my own physical limitations, and a gate that I can't open on my own. I'm stuck. By myself there is nothing I can do. I look up, and there is a loving Father. He knows I can't climb; He knows I'm trapped. But He is Love, and He can't leave me there. He has to come down the stairs and open the gate and pick me up in His arms. And then, wrapped in His love, I'll have nothing left to cry about.

All I did was let Him know I wanted to be with Him, and He was there. Nothing else I could do would help me climb those stairs. He bent down, and did it all, because He couldn't bear to leave me there, either.

Dear Father, thank You for reaching down and lifting me up. Help me to realize that it is only in Your love and strength that I can climb closer to You, and help me not to depend on myself. Without You I am much too weak. I love You, and want to be with You at the top of those stairs, forever. Amen.

Is there any area in your life where you have been trying to depend upon your own weak strength, instead of depending upon God's omnipotence? What can you do about it?

Children are happiest when they are close to their parents.

What can you do today so that you can all enjoy being close for a while?

If you are feeling sad, like a bereft child at the bottom of the stairs, imagine God's coming down to you, sweeping you up in His arms, and loving you until there are no more tears left. How does that image make you feel?

Things that go bump!

Today an old friend called me on the phone, and, while we chatted, Joel and Nathan played cars on the living room floor. Nathan had put a play mat on the floor, with roads and farms printed on it, and he lined up all his cars, bumper to bumper, till they filled every inch of road and created a major traffic-flow crisis. Nathan, at 4, is a precise child. Every car has to be in its proper place. Joel is eleven months old, and at the 'chuck and look' stage of babyhood. As far as he is concerned, objects are designed to be thrown as far as possible, and then you look to see where they went. It's even better if the action also makes a good loud noise.

Nathan likes Joel, and is fairly tolerant of the chaos that erupts whenever he is around, but, eventually, his patience wears thin, and he drags Joel unceremoniously through the house and dumps him at my feet. Inside a chubby little hand is a little metal car. Joel wanders away from me and starts banging the car on different surfaces to see which will make the loudest noise. He tries the floor, the sofa, Nathan's head (that makes an interesting sound!), and winds up at a little antiqued-pine table. Before I can grab him he bangs the car down on the wooden surface. He manages to repeat this several times before I can finally finish my telephone conversation.

I whisk Joel up in my arms and prevent a further assault on the little table, a home-coming gift when Nathan was born. There are six or so obvious dents in the surface. In another corner is a deep score mark made by an over-enthusiastic penciller. There's a water mark from a glass of juice, and several other scratches on the legs where other toy cars were involved in near-fatal accidents.

One day, when there are no longer any carefree little hands and bodies playing in our home, I'll look at the little bumps and scratches with fond memories of the fun of tiny children.

My body has also taken the toll of bearing three children, two of whom were well over nine pounds (4kg). I have permanent scars — stretch marks in places I never knew you could get them. Sometimes in the shower I look at my crinkles, and wistfully wish I could iron them smooth. But the thought doesn't last for long. Stretch marks and bumps on the furniture are a small price to pay for the delight of our children and a loving and happily chaotic home!

Jesus bears some scars too. Scars that will never go away. Scars that show His sacrifice for us. He considered them a small price to pay, so that He could share the delight of His children for eternity. And He'll bear those scars for ever to remind us how much He loves us.

Dear Father, thank You for the scars on Your Son which let me know how much I am loved by You. Help me share Your love with others, knowing that their feelings are more important than how my house looks. Amen.

Think of some of the bumps and scars on your home and your family members. Which one evokes the happiest memory? . . . the saddest memory? . . . the craziest memory?

Do you know anyone with whom you can share God's love this week? Show someone else that their feelings are more important than the appearance of your house.

What are some positive ways to respond to a child who has accidentally damaged something in your home?

Making friends for eternity

I was working in the kitchen when I overheard two little girls talking in the next room.

'Kirsty, do you love Jesus?'

'I don't really know. I don't know much about Him.'

'You have to love Jesus if you want to go to heaven, and I want you to be in heaven too.' Bethany was getting concerned.

'What if I told Jesus I was your sister? Would they let me in then?'

A long, thoughtful pause.

'No, that wouldn't work.'

'Why not?'

'Well, because that would be a lie, and you can't go to heaven if you tell lies.'

Kirsty's mother smoked. Whenever Bethany saw Kirsty's Mum she would tell her to stop smoking because it wasn't good for her health, and it didn't smell very nice, either.

At 4, Bethany was so concerned about our neighbour's children that she wrapped up an old Christian story-book and pushed it through their letter-box.

At 6 she found another friend who didn't know much about Jesus; so she invited her along to our family worship once a week. Last week Bethany prayed that Sarah would be able to come to church with us soon.

It must be wonderful to be young and free of the inhibitions that come with adulthood. Bethany goes where I fear to tread, and says what I would hesitate to say. She is straightforward, clear and honest. She is so concerned about the eternal prospects of her friends.

It puts me to shame. I am naturally a shy person, and not very assertive with others. I prefer to build up relationships slowly, and wait till there is trust and credibility, before telling others about my faith in a loving God.

But Bethany just goes right ahead. Almost as soon as she has made friends she finds out whether or not they love Jesus. She can't bear the thought of anyone she knows being 'lost'.

Maybe God has other ways for me to share His love with my friends. Maybe it's OK to witness in a different way. I write articles for a Christian outreach magazine, and, by doing so, I can touch people I'll never meet. But if I can call up a friend and tell her the good news that spaghetti sauce is at a low price in the supermarket, or I've found out where to buy the edible seaweed she was looking for, then why don't I always feel so comfortable telling her the good news that Jesus loves and forgives her? First I need to feel that overwhelming concern for the happiness of each of my friends, just as Bethany does.

Now I know why it is so important to become as little children . . . . My friend's life may depend on it.

Dear Father, I love You and I want to share Your love with others. Sometimes my feelings and inhibitions get in the way. Give me the courage I need to tell my friends about the peace and joy I have found in You. Amen.

How do you find it easiest to share Jesus' love?

Is there someone you can witness to today?

Write down a few of the ways God has helped you recently, and then try to share some of these events with your friends in a natural and relaxed manner.

Close to His heart

When Joel was small I used to carry him around in a baby sling, snuggled close to my chest, so that I still had two hands free to do all the housework, or to do something with the other two children. I liked to feel his tiny body, peacefully resting against my own. When he grew too big for the sling, he went into the backpack carrier, and peered over my shoulder as I walked around. Occasionally I would hear a tired sigh, and then feel a gentle 'bump' as a drowsy child finally succumbed to sleep, and his head fell to rest on my back.

'You'll regret this,' an older woman warned. 'You should teach them to stay in their play-pens while you work, and they need to learn how to go to sleep on their own. You don't want to carry that child around with you all the time.' She shrugged her shoulders and left, shaking her head.

I felt guilty. It's a good job she doesn't know that Joel sleeps all night in my arms as well, I thought. Was I really such a bad mother because I didn't discipline my child to be alone? I did admire and envy those mums who seemed to 'have it all together', and had babies who slept twelve hours a night in their own little cots. And it would be bliss to have a full night of sleep without being woken by little Jojo every couple of hours! Maybe he was becoming spoilt after all? We had tried to encourage the boys to sleep through the night in their own cots, but they could both scream for hours, until, shattered and exhausted, we had to pacify them anyway so that we could all have at least a few hours' rest. We were glad that we had an extra-wide bed!

When all the modern experts of child-care bombard me with information about all the things I'm supposed to do, I have a great, secret delight in thinking back a few thousand years and imagining what mothers would have done then, and probably still do in most places in the world. I imagine mothers working with their babies tied to their backs, and sleeping on mats, with their babies all cuddled up close to them. I don't envision play-pens, and cots shut away in distant rooms. And I tell myself that babies need to be near their mothers — that's what God intended. I think these things to salve my conscience — but there are times when I am tired of carrying a fussy child in one arm while I try to cook the dinner. There are nights when I just want to sleep, and his constant feeding drives me crazy. Sometimes the left side of my back aches because I always carry Joel over my left arm.

I once read that the more physical contact a child has with his mother, the more intelligent he is likely to be. A child in an orphanage without love and cuddles is less likely to develop well intellectually, and may even regress. If that is true, then all my children should be geniuses!

I also read that if you are physically 'there' for your child, every time he needs you when he is a baby, then he will not be so demanding as he grows older. Nathan was an extremely clingy baby for the first fourteen months, then suddenly he took off! He still likes lots of hugs, but now he plays happily by himself for hours.

As a mum, however tired or busy you are, it's a wonderful feeling when a child comes running to you, smiling, for a great big hug, and then, just as suddenly, runs off to do something else fun. It's great to be needed, and wanted, and loved and cuddled, and I tell myself that I may not always be there to hug them when they need it, and one day they may not be there to hug either, so I want to make the most of the closeness while they're still here and huggable!

I know that for years God has carried me around, close to His heart, even when I was oblivious, and 'sleeping'. And now that I am aware of His presence, I know I am happiest, too, when I'm in close contact with my Father. The closer we are to Him, day and night, the more we develop spiritually, and the stronger we become. When we know He will always be there for us, it gives us the courage to try new adventures and take new risks for Him.

Dear Father, thank You for carrying me and my family close to Your heart. May Your arms be the most wonderful place for us to be, now and forever. Amen.

Sit quietly for a few minutes, and imagine that you are sitting in God's lap, and He has His arms around you. Just rest in His love and peace for a few quiet and warm moments. Then reach up and whisper in His ear, and tell Him just how much you love Him.

Take some time today to give each of your children a big, close hug, and listen, really listen to the little things they have to say to you.

How does it make you feel to know that God is carrying your children close to His heart, too?

Storm on the mountain

'I think we ought to turn back now,' Bernie said. 'It sounds as if a storm is coming.' It was lovely up there on the mountain. We had come up the gentle way for the children's sake, riding the ski-lift, swinging up over the Alpine meadows sprinkled with spring flowers, accompanied by the soft music of distant cowbells. It had been idyllic. Then we had hiked on, farther up the mountain, for better views and the refreshing taste of an Alpine waterfall. But the rumble of thunder reminded us that we didn't have all day, and neither had we brought our 'emergency' bag of snacks, waterproofs, and first-aid supplies.

The children were relieved to turn round; at 3 and 6 they were young and tiring of the walk. Baby Joel was riding on his daddy's back. As we walked back down we noticed that the restaurant by the lift was strangely deserted. I wondered why. Then my heart stopped with a sickening realization. The little chairs dangling in the sky were stock still. The ski-lift had closed for the day. We were stranded high in the Alps with no food, no waterproofs, three small children and an approaching storm.

There was a path down to the car park, but we had no idea how far it would be. It could be several miles of zigzagging pathways. We knew we had to get down, but the children were already tired. Revived by the promise of an ice-cream, we began to hurry along the rocky pathway. Five minutes later the storm broke. We rushed for a little mountain hut, hoping it would be open for shelter, but it was locked. We huddled against the leeward side of the hut, children screaming, rain pelting through our summer clothing, thunder crashing and lightning ripping the air only feet away. It was a living nightmare. In minutes we were drenched, and then the hail came. Baby Joel had sat in his backpack, smiling at the rain pouring over his face, but he began yelling, too, as the hail dashed against his bare and hairless head. The ice chilled us to the bone as we tried to protect our terrified children between our bodies and the hut wall. For a moment I had visions of being stranded there all night: hypothermia, pneumonia and absolute misery.

A text came into my mind, 'He gently leads those that have young,' Isaiah 40:11. 'Lord,' I prayed, 'I need some gentle leading now. Please help us! The children are tired and cold, scared and hungry, wet and miserable, and so am I. Please help the storm to stop . . . . PS: Please make it stop within the next five minutes! Amen.'

Bernie had been praying, too. We began to sing to try and make ourselves feel more cheerful and confident. Suddenly we realized the storm had stopped. We yelled with delight, and headed back to the path . . . but it was now a torrent of water flooding down the mountainside. We couldn't walk on it, so we had to trudge through deep fields of slithery hailstones, our feet numb with the cold. We had to take Joel out of the backpack, and I held him close to my body, so he would keep warm. I had no free hands to save myself if I should slip on the mud and hail. Bernie had Nathan and Bethany clinging to his hands. They were both crying and struggling, shivering and soaked to the skin. Bernie had the hardest job because if one fell, they all would. The children sobbed almost all the way down the mountain path.

The rain held off until we got back to the main road,

and reached a small bus-shelter. Bernie ran on to fetch the car. We had been drenched in ice-cold water for over an hour. 'Oh, no,' I thought aloud, 'I hope we don't spend the rest of our trip sick with chills!' 'Of course we won't, Mummy,' said Bethany. 'Up there I prayed that no one would get hurt or ill, so I know we're all going to be all right!' Minutes later they were begging for ice-creams — but, for once in my life, I decided not to join them! We all had hot showers and soup, and soon recovered from our ordeal, and not one of us had a cough or a sneeze!

God 'gently leads those that have young'. He knows we are more vulnerable when we have to care of His little lambs. He understands that we may not be able to travel as far, as fast, or over such difficult terrain. So He leads us tenderly, and softly. He stands by to ease our burdens, and to be there whenever we need Him. And when the pressures of parenthood seem to hammer us into the ground, He is there to carry our little lambs, and their parents, through the storm, and into the sunshine.

Dear Father, thank You for understanding that, as parents, we have to care for our little lambs, and we need gentle pastures. Thank You for being our loving Shepherd, over the mountains, and through the valleys. Amen.

Think of a time when you have experienced God's gentle leading through a difficult situation as a mother.

Read Psalm 23, and rewrite it, paraphrasing it to suit your own personal needs.

Or read Psalm 23 and list all the ways God takes care of you in your present situation.

Why tarantulas are always female

'Mummy, tarantulas are always lady spiders, aren't they?' Nathan's interest in creepy-crawlies had been aroused ever since he could crawl fast enough to catch one of the wood-lice that would occasionally venture across our living-room carpet. At first he was just interested in their flavour, and how squishy they were, but, fortunately, the desire to catch them for food soon waned. Now, at 4, he would pore over pictures of insects for hours. Grandma had found a wonderful book of pop-up insects that hopped off the pages, and were gigantic wonders of paper engineering. As far as Nathan was concerned, tarantulas were truly beautiful — and always female.

'Why do you think they are all ladies?' I asked.

'Because they have long hair, of course!' Of course — how could I have been so stupid!

We were in a hotel with Bethany, when a group of people came into the lounge and began to chat and smoke.

'Mummy, Mummy! Why has that lady got a candle stuck in her mouth?'

'What does Pastor Bernie do for a job?' A little boy asked Nathan at a church picnic. My ears pricked up — this should be interesting, I thought!

'I don't know.' Nathan looked thoughtful. 'He talks a lot.'

'Is that all?' David seemed incredulous.

'I don't know — I suppose so.'

'Wow! I want to do that when I grow up!'

'Mummy, what's it like for the baby in your tummy?' I was seven months pregnant with Joel, and Nathan was sitting on the five inches left of my lap.

'Well, it's dark, and cosy, and comfortable, and the baby has its own specially warm swimming pool to play around in.'

Nathan slid off and went to play in his paddling pool. The water was cold, so he soon jumped out again.

'Mummy, when the baby's finished with your swimming pool, can I have a go?'

It's lovely being with children and finding out how they see their world. Their perspectives are fresh, funny, interesting, and innocent. You can see how their little minds have tried so hard to work something out for themselves, based on the limits of their experience and understanding.

Nearly every day, when I pray, I try to imagine what God is like. The children ask questions about what it's like in heaven, and I do my best to answer them. Things happen, and I try to work out why. But I can understand and explain them only from my own very limited, and inadequate, experience. One day I shall see Him face to face, and then everything will be made clear. In the meantime, I'm sure the things I say, every now and then, must bring a little smile to His perfect face.

Dear Father, thank You for sending me Your Holy Spirit to explain things, and help me to understand. Forgive me for the times when my 'explanations' and ideas are so completely inadequate or laughable. Help me to understand more of Your beautiful character, and Your plan for me, day by day. Amen.

Think of a funny time when one of your children offered a childlike explanation.

Think of ways in which your picture of God, and what He does, has matured and altered with time and experience.

Is there a passage in the Bible or some aspect of theology that you have found difficult to understand? Have another go at studying the topic, asking the Holy Spirit to explain it to you. Ask your pastor for help, or find a study guide in your Christian book store that helps to clarify what you want to discover.

Angels and vanilla puddles

I believe in angels. As a mother, it is a necessity. I can't be with each child all the time. I don't really have eyes in the back of my head — just an awareness of those strange, suspicious silences which mean that something is going on somewhere that probably shouldn't be happening! As with baby Joel — he enjoys chewing toilet brushes, digging up house plants, dropping pieces of his toys into the kitchen bin, and running around the house with the loose end of toilet paper rolls!

It's a great comfort to know that watching over three active, inquisitive, experimental children isn't all down to Bernie and me. We've done what we can — the toilet brush is kept on the window sill; the toilet lid 'locks'; we have stair-gates on the stairs, safety catches on the windows, and cupboard and drawer locks all over the kitchen. I can put up with these little inconveniences for the sake of a little extra peace of mind. But I'm glad there are angels too. They can be everywhere we can't be; they don't get tired; they can use supernatural powers.

Recently I was cooking in the kitchen and Joel was playing on the floor. I had to leave the room for a minute or two when suddenly I heard a yell. I dashed back into the room. Joel was sitting in a large puddle of brown liquid that seemed to cover half the floor. A large bottle with its bottom missing lay in the flood, with chunks of jagged glass protruding like icebergs out of a brown sea. Joel was still yelling and sitting in the puddle. I picked him up to check him for cuts. I couldn't see anything visible, so I pulled off his clothes. There was so much brown liquid around, it was hard to tell whether or not he was bleeding.

Fortunately there wasn't a scratch on him. I must have left a cupboard door ajar so that its lock hadn't engaged. Joel had pulled out a brand new, one pint bottle of vanilla essence, and dropped it on the floor. The kitchen, and Joel, have been beautifully fragrant ever since.

I cleaned up the mess, and carried on. For a few hours I was preoccupied with cooking, then, with the kitchen still warm, and with the cooling racks piled high with goodies, I had a rare few minutes to sit and ponder while the children were playing happily. I thought back over the day: the vanilla puddle, the broken glass; and suddenly I realized how much danger Joel had faced. He had walked and sat in that puddle, full of jagged pieces of glass. He likes to pick things up, and he could have easily tried to grab at the bits on the floor. It was a miracle he wasn't hurt when he'd dropped the bottle in the first place.

I paused, and prayed. And I thanked God, once again, for angels.

Dear Father, thank You for Your loving protection. Thank You for angels to help me watch over my children. Amen.

List a few times when you believe that angels have protected you and your children from danger.

Tell your children a story about angel protection, preferably one from your own experience.

Help the little ones make an angel mobile or picture to hang in their bedrooms to remind them that they have special guardian angels who watch over them all the time.

As different as snowflakes

By the time our second child was a few days old we discovered, much to our immense surprise, that all children are different! Some scream all the time; some feed all the time, some throw up all the time (well, maybe not all the time; it just feels that way!) And some babies are supposed to sleep all the time. (Oh, what bliss!)

One of the most frustrating things about parenting the second time around is that after lots of trial and error, and a good deal of practice on number one, we feel that we have this whole parenting thing pretty much under control. When Bethany was tiny it would take me half an hour to change her; now I can do a change in five minutes, even a messy one. Looking back, I think it took me much longer to get Bethany ready in the morning than it now takes to change, wash and dress all three children!

As soon as Bethany's little teeth began to show above the gums, like snowdrops pushing through, I felt it was important to clean them properly. I bought a tiny pink toothbrush and special baby toothpaste. I smiled a lot and told her it would be fun, just like a little tickle in her mouth . . . . I made up stories about the kitten printed on the handle . . . . I tried songs and funny rhymes . . . . I tried different flavours of toothpaste: strawberry, mint, orange . . . . (I even found one flavoured with bubble-gum, but I couldn't bring myself to buy it!) I tried using a mirror . . . . I even let her try to clean *my* teeth . . . . She was not one bit impressed. As far as she was concerned no one, but no one, was going to get a toothbrush into her mouth. The mere sight of the thing made her clench her jaws together, and nothing could prise them apart. Eventually she would cry, and we'd get the brush in quickly, and clean as best we could.

Nathan wasn't overly impressed with toothbrushes, either, but, even before he had teeth, Joel would pull the toothbrushes out of our mouths, and scrub his gums with them. He would wander off and hide toothbrushes in obscure places, much to the amusement of the other children, and our frequent frustration! Almost nothing excited him as much as a toothbrush. He would sit and scrub his gums when he was teething. No plastic rings for him, not even ones filled with chilled water! He just loved chewing toothbrushes, especially if they weren't his!

Bethany would make friends with anyone, wherever we were. Nathan would dive under my skirts if anyone so much as looked at him. Bethany would sleep through the night. Nathan and Joel still don't. Bethany loves books; Nathan loves designing machines, and Joel treats the world as one huge joke.

We are all different; as different as snowflakes. It helps to create a much more interesting world, and helps us learn about tolerance, and acceptance. It's wonderful to watch each child, each new life, unfold and develop, revealing new traits, skills, and ideas. As a parent you quickly learn that you can't treat all your children in exactly the same way. Some need gentle restraint, while others need a gentle push. Some need a bit of direction; others are best left to work things out for themselves. For one child, sitting quietly for a few minutes is a terrible punishment. For another, it is bliss! The tricky bit, for parents, is discovering the pattern for each little snowflake.

Being a mum has helped me to understand why God

treats us all differently. He knows us better than we know ourselves. He watched us grow before we were even born. He can see inside our personalities and lives, and He knows exactly how to respond to each one of us. He knows the best way to communicate with us, and guide us. He knows what is going to be best for us in the long run. We have to trust that He is being fair to each one of us, in ways far beyond our current level of comprehension.

Dear Father, thank You for creating us with such variety. Please help me understand the complexities of my children's personalities, so that I can communicate with them, and guide them in the most appropriate ways. Help me to trust that You are working everything out for my good, through the ups and through the downs. Amen.

How can you treat your children differently and still be fair?

Think about a time in your life when you felt God wasn't treating you fairly, but later you discovered that He had done the best thing possible for you.

How can you help someone you know who thinks that God is treating him badly?

The tale of two gravestones

The raspy breathing of baby Joel woke me from my shallow sleep. All night his breathing had been noisy, interspersed with hacking coughs, and moans, and cries. He was sleeping in my arms so I could comfort him, and stroke him, and rub his back, but his breathing was becoming worse, and I recognized the symptoms of croup. Nathan had cut each tooth with a mild bout of croup, so we were used to the routine. I dragged myself wearily out of bed, picked Joel up and wrapped him in his shawl. First we went to the open window and let him breathe a few breaths of chilly night air. I know it sounds strange, but that's what we had been told to do. The cold air helps to constrict the blood vessels, and prevent further congestion. Then I took him downstairs to boil the kettle and fill the kitchen with steam for him to breathe. Half an hour of steam, and his breathing had become easier; he had fallen asleep, and I climbed wearily up the stairs and back into bed.

Maybe our children only suffer from mild bouts of croup, or maybe, by recognizing the symptoms and treating them early, the problems don't become too serious. I don't know. But I pray my way through every episode, praying for wisdom to do the right thing, praying for the health of my tiny, vulnerable children as they struggle for breath, praying for their lives, and finally praying thanks for their safe recovery.

On the Isle of Wight, just off the south coast of England, there is a little village church in an ancient churchyard. In the heart of that cemetery, filled with mossy, time-eroded stones, I found a tragic story of a mother's struggle. A tiny grave with one headstone. Four little girls aged from 1 to 8 died within ten days. The stone said that they had all died from croup. My vivid imagination pictured the agony of a mother watching her children die, helpless, as she held them in her arms as their breathing became more laboured. A praying, crying, desperate mother, becoming more desperate with the loss of each beautiful daughter. I could only imagine the depth of her sorrow, her despair, a heart broken four times in two handfuls of days. As I stood by that headstone, worn by 150 years of sea breezes, my own heart broke for the long-ago mother.

Finally I pulled myself away, and went on to the next stone, that of a young woman, not even 30. Another tragedy. And then I noticed something else. This stone was a sequel to the first. The grave of the young mother, with a broken heart. Three months of profound grief was all she could bear, and then she joined her four little girls under the island sod.

The tragedy seemed to be amplified by the fact that a simple solution could have prevented such intense sorrow: a steamy kettle in the middle of the night. Maybe she had no idea what to do; maybe she didn't realize how easily she could ease the suffering of her little ones. Maybe it wasn't croup after all, but actually diphtheria; in those days there was often confusion about the actual cause of death.

Today many people are dying, tragically unaware of the simple solution that could save their lives, bringing them forgiveness, acceptance, peace and comfort, hope and joy. Jesus is waiting, knocking on the door, with all the help they need. The solution is so close to hand, but they just don't realize it.

If I had lived on the Isle of Wight 150 years ago I would have wanted, more than anything else, to share the simple treatment for croup with a young mother. If I hadn't, I'd have felt responsible in some way for the loss of those little lives . . . . But maybe there are people I'll meet today in need of simple solutions to save their souls for eternity. What shall I share with them?

Dear Father, thank You for sending Jesus to teach me how to live so that I will not have to die. Thank You for the simple 'cure' You have provided for my own sin-sickness. I love You. Amen.

How can you share the good news about Jesus with someone in your world today?

What 'tip' have you found to be a 'life-saver' in your experience? Can you share the good advice with someone else?

Are there people whom you would like to see in heaven, who do not know Jesus yet? Pray for them every day, and find ways to share Jesus' love with them as often as you can.

Aprons and potato peelings

It's hard to find time to pray when you're a mother. I have great admiration for Susannah Wesley, mother of the famous Wesleys, and about eighteen other children. She managed to homeschool all of them, even though she must have been continually pregnant! Rumours say that whenever she wanted to pray she threw her voluminous apron over her head, and then the children knew they had to be quiet and not make a disturbance. She is even supposed to have taught her children to cry quietly! Maybe Susannah Wesley was the model for the Proverbs 31 lady! Or maybe the mists of time have blurred reality. Or maybe she really was so closely in touch with God. I look forward to catching up with her in heaven one day, when she will be able to pray without that large, white apron!

I try not to get out of bed until I have prayed and spent time with God. Bernie is very sensitive to this — he knows what I'm like to live with if I don't start the day with God! And even when I do get time with God, by the time Bethany and Nathan have left for school, I'm usually in need of a few more prayers!

So Bernie gets up and washes the children, and supervises their dressing. Their school has a uniform: burgundy, grey and white in winter, with pink gingham dresses for the girls in summer.

The uniform is supposed to minimize hassle, but my prayers are often interrupted by the patter of little feet, who try to tiptoe quietly into my room so as not to disturb me. Then I hear the whisper, 'Mummy, I want to wear my Mickey Mouse socks today, so I can show them to Simon when we have gym. Where are they?' They are usually hanging up to dry somewhere, in the bottom of the laundry basket, or stuffed, by Joel, down someone's boot. I'm trying to pray for Bernie's study group.

Then Bethany creeps in. 'Mummy,' she whispers, 'did you remember that you said you'd find the book on recycling for me? I need it for science class today.' No, I didn't remember, and it's probably in the attic, in one of the several dozen apple boxes stored under the eaves. I go back to praying for Mrs Jones's gall-bladder operation. And I ask God to help me find the book quickly, before Bethany has to leave for school.

Then Joel breaks loose from Bernie, while Daddy's trying to look for the Mickey Mouse socks. He comes in yelling, climbs into bed, and hurls himself at me for a hug. What can I do? I hug him, and struggle to keep him still and quiet while I try to finish my prayer time. I often have to end with an 'I'm afraid I'll have to go now, but I'll try to catch up with You again later. Amen.' And I'm sure God understands — but later may not come until eleven o'clock at night, or it may have to wait until tomorrow.

So often it seems hard enough, as a mum, to pray for a minute, let alone 'without ceasing'! But a few things can help us spend more time with God. One is to pray for a different category of requests each day: yourself one day, your spouse the next, then your children, other relatives, friends and neighbours, your church and your church family, then missions and outreach, and finally world issues, or something along those lines. This way our prayers can be less repetitive and time-consuming, and we can concentrate more specifically on the details.

Make a prayer list, and keep it in your handbag, or even the nappy bag, and pray in odd moments: waiting at check-outs, sitting in the doctor's surgery, or moving in slow traffic. Stick a prayer list on the fridge door, or a bathroom mirror, and each time you look there, pray for the next thing on the list. Another idea is to link a prayer theme with different household chores — pray for Mrs Jones's gall-bladder whenever you do the vacuuming; Katie's baby when you do the dishes; a new outreach contact whenever you peel potatoes, etc.

As mothers we are always going to be interrupted. It's hard to say to an eager child, 'Please go away and be quiet — I'm trying to pray now.' Children's prayers are short and said out loud, and it's hard for them to relate to a mother's silent praying for longer than one minute. I even remember saying, 'Mummy needs to pray right now — if she doesn't pray she'll be even crabbier than she normally is!' Once, when Nathan insisted on being close to me when I was praying, I hugged him, and prayed out loud, so he could hear the kinds of things I prayed about, and he could hear that I prayed for him, too. After that, he seemed to interrupt my prayers less often, because he understood more about what was happening inside of me.

You have to find what works best for you. It's great if Daddy can help out and give you an island of prayerful peace in each day. But daddies are not always around. Maybe you could pray when your children are having a nap. Let them play in the garden, and sit out there with them, while you pray. It's OK to pray while they watch one of their favourite Bible videos, or a good TV show. Or push them out in their buggies, and get some fresh air and exercise as you talk to God. One brave mother even prayed that God would wake her each night at 2am to pray, because the house was always quiet at that time. He answered her prayer, and she says that she was never tired because of the lost sleep!

It's wonderful if children will learn to respect your prayer time, but, if you are interrupted, that's OK; God understands; He knows all you have to cram into the day, and that you'll get back to Him when you can. Or maybe you need to buy that large, white, linen apron, after all!

Dear Father, thank You for prayer. It is such a wonderfully easy way to be in contact with You and heaven. It's good to be able to pray any time, anywhere, and about anything. Help me to find time to pray, and to learn how to pray effectively. Help me to find time to listen to You speaking in my life, too. Amen.

Write out a prayer list for each day of the week, under seven separate headings, such as family, friends, self, church, relatives, world issues, outreach, etc. Keep it; review it regularly, and note any thoughts or answers you may have.

Or use a diary, and write something special you have prayed for each day. Leave some space to add other thoughts, and answers to your prayers, as they come.

Divine service?

'Mummy, Mummy, please can you wipe my nose!' I'd heard the words repeated about every five minutes during the day. Three-year-old Nathan had a cold. The requests for nose wiping were interspersed with other requests. 'Mummy, Mummy, please will you wipe my bottom!' 'Mummy, Mummy, please can I have a drink of water!' I decided life might be simpler if I tied a roll of bathroom tissue around my neck, as our Kleenex supply was being quickly depleted.

Bethany needed her shoes finding for school, and at the last minute she remembered she had to take any spare house bricks along for a special project! Joel had a mild tummy-upset and I had to change his nappy almost every hour. In between these major essentials I was mopping small patches of Joel's vomit off the carpet; rinsing, washing and hanging the cloth nappies up to dry; nursing the baby; trying to make lunch, and prepare for dinner; answer the telephone; and do the ironing.

I had a 'to do' list for the week which I'd pared down to the absolute essentials. It was already Thursday and I hadn't managed to tackle any of them — even something as small as writing a birthday card for a friend! And then Bernie checked his diary, and we found out that it was our turn to clean the church. A couple of friends called us to say they desperately needed to come and see us for the weekend, and there was barely time to get to the supermarket, even though it was so close we could see it from our house!

I hurtled from one mini-crisis to the next, longing for a break. Just a few minutes to sit and sew something beautiful. I wanted to do something that wouldn't need doing again a few minutes later. I wanted to taste the luxury of doing something totally indulgent and non-essential! I wanted to do something relaxing to soothe my harassed nerves. I believed in spending at least ten minutes a day doing something creative, but, as I crashed into bed at midnight, with lots of jobs still to do, I realized such ideals would have to wait till the following week, or the week after, or maybe the following year!

We barely made it to church that week. Arriving in a chaotic heap of nappy bags, 'happy bags' to help keep the children content during Daddy's sermon, and a box of stuff, grabbed almost at the last minute, to help me with the children's Bible classes.

As I collapsed into a back pew in a dishevelled heap of baggage and babies, I hoped for a peaceful hour. Baby Joel would probably sleep; and I had lots of things to help keep the children quiet during the service. They were always pretty good in church.

Five minutes into the service Joel began to fuss. Suddenly he was explosively sick. I grabbed a cloth to try to clean up the mess, but more was to follow. He was plastered in cheesy milk; I had it in my hair and all down my dress. There was some on the carpet, too. I frantically began rubbing, mopping and wiping, still holding a very miserable Joel. Then I went out to the kitchen to try to find a damp cloth, and he was sick again.

By that time we both needed a good bath. I'd had enough of struggling. I swept the children out of church, gathered up the bags and drove back home. Bernie could have a ride with our visitors.

I let the children watch Bible videos, bathed Joel and myself, and flopped into a chair. Joel soon went to sleep. I sat for a while, just feeling the peace. Then I prayed:

'Dear Father, I long to do something special for You, to find some way to serve You. Right now it seems hard to see beyond these four walls. All my time is filled up with caring for these little ones, these lovely gifts from You. Help me to see where I can serve You too. Amen.'

And, in the pause that followed, my heart heard His Spirit say, 'All these things, these caring things that help your children feel happy and comfortable, all these things say to Me "I love you, and your needs are important to me". And every time you do one of these little things, you are showing Me your love too. I know some things are messy, or time-consuming, and I know you often think it would be great to achieve wonderful things for Me, and serve Me in a special way, but this is service too, and it's the most beautiful service in the world. I remember each sacrificial, serving moment of motherhood in just the way I remember when Mary bathed my feet with perfume, and wiped them with her hair.

'I tell you the truth: whatever you did for one of the least of these brothers of mine, you did for me.'

Dear Father, help me to see the mundane activities that fill my life as ways in which I can serve You, too. Help me to feel that what I do is valuable in Your sight, and help me to serve cheerfully, even when I feel frustrated and exhausted. Thank You. Amen.

How does it help you to see that what you are doing, in your everyday life, is serving God, too?

Someone has said that motherhood is the most important job in the world. What do you think?

Plan a few minutes today to take some time for yourself, and do something you enjoy. You will feel happier, and more content, if you can plan for this time, and it will help you serve more effectively, too.

Just watching!

I was preparing dinner in the kitchen. Bethany was playing on the computer in the office. Nathan was redesigning British Rail in the living room, and Joel had been bashing an old pot with a wooden spoon, but was now wobbling round and round my left leg. This was fine, until I had to move to reach the sink, or open the refrigerator, then Joel lost his balance, or I tripped over him, or both. The casserole was baking; the potatoes were done; the salad had been tossed; what else did we need? Oh, yes, the frozen peas.

The kitchen is one of the smallest rooms in our house. It used to be a bit bigger, but a previous owner had turned the original, large kitchen into a dining room, and built a new kitchen on to the back of the house. 'Compact and efficient' was how the house particulars described it. I could stand in the middle and reach virtually everything. There was a tiny space for a refrigerator under the work surface. We had to take out a cupboard to make a space for the washing machine, the microwave sat on the dishwasher, and there was no room for the freezer. We could have put it upstairs in Bethany's room, but I finally persuaded Bernie to hide it in the garage.

Having the freezer in the garage has a few advantages. One is that it's easier to defrost — excess water just drips onto the garage floor. It's also out of the way, and it's handy if you fancy an ice cream while changing the spark plugs. One disadvantage is that there is nowhere safe and clean to put a baby when you're busy digging a lost pie out of the 'snow'. Another disadvantage is that Nathan thinks it's funny to shut the front door when Mummy is outside, so I have to take my keys with me, just in case his mischief, or a gusty breeze, leaves me stranded.

To get the peas, I would have to leave Joel indoors when I went out to the freezer. I needed to fetch bread and other things for supper at the same time, and my arms would be full.

'Nathan, I'm just going out to the freezer for a minute. Please can you watch Joel for me? I'll just sit him over here where he can see you. Thanks, darling.'

I couldn't have been gone longer than a couple of minutes. As I re-entered the house Nathan called, 'Mummy! Mummy! Come and see what Joel's done!' My heart sank. I dropped the freezer things, and ran into the living room. Joel was sitting in the middle of a pile of earth and leaves, shoving handfuls of potting compost into his grimy little mouth.

'Oh, Nathan! I thought you were watching Joel for me!'

'I was, Mummy! It was really funny! You should have seen how he climbed on my books and then the plant fell all over him! And he ate the dirt, too! It must have been really yucky!' Nathan was obviously delighted by Joel's performance.

As I cleaned up the mess, and repotted the dishevelled-looking weeping fig, I thought about Nathan. It wasn't his fault. Maybe it was my use of language. After all, he *watches* television. He *watches* the birds. He was just *watching* Joel. *Watching* didn't mean that he had to *do* anything about what he saw happen. Watching was a passive amusement rather than an activity.

God asks us to be 'watchful'. Not just to be passive onlookers, an indifferent audience, but to act positively on what we see happening in our own lives, the world around us, and the people we meet each day. We aren't here to watch while disaster strikes and people get themselves into a real mess. We are here to watch as protectors, knowing the potential dangers that others don't realize exist, dangers with eternal implications. We are to be aware, to help create safe environments, and prevent ourselves, and other people, having to face calamities.

'Watching' the world is challenging. There are so many disasters and dangers that we can be overwhelmed by the number of people who need our help. So God does not just say 'Watch', He says, 'Devote yourselves to prayer', because when we pray we have all the positive power in the universe at our fingertips. Prayer combines perfectly with watching to help us protect ourselves and others. And, finally, He reminds us to be thankful too, and praise Him for the ways He protects and guides us through the minefield of life.

Dear Father, help me to have the courage to be truly 'watchful' in my own life, and in the lives of those around me. Give me the wisdom and the love to reach out and help to prevent personal disasters. Thank You for watching over me, and my family. Amen.

Have you been 'watching' anyone you know come close to a personal disaster? Have you been able to do anything to try to help prevent the problem?

Pray for your friends whose families and lives seem to be heading for difficulties.

Think of ways in which you can reach out and care for someone you know who is going through a crisis right now, or who has experienced one recently.

Oh, no! It's mealtime again!

One of the greatest frustrations of my life is encouraging my children to eat healthy food. We have vegetarian children who don't like vegetables! I am bored with eating the same few meals that they will eat happily, but can't face the trauma of introducing something new only to have a battle of a mealtime, be told it's 'yucky', and then have to throw most of it away! So we stick to the few faithfuls; spaghetti and nut balls, pizza, Vegeburgers, pasta in sauce, and a few other things. Occasionally I get brave and make a quiche, or something else 'exotic'. Often I make a big pot of lentil soup because they like that, and it covers over a multitude of wonderful vegetables once it has been through the blender. Then, for several days, we will just have bread and soup for dinner. It's quick, easy, just as nourishing as a main course, and there are no complaints — it's a wonder we don't eat soup every day!

It's not that we haven't tried. There has always been good food on the table. We've always encouraged the children to try at least a little bit of everything. One child expert tells us not to make meals a battlefield because we need to save our strength and relationships for more important battles in parenting. A traditionalist expects children to eat everything on their plates. Another 'expert' says it's not worth the aggravation — just give them the few things they'll eat happily; be glad they're eating something, and put up with boring meals for the next twenty years!

Bethany loves savoury pies; Nathan will eat only the pastry. Nathan loves corn-on-the-cob; Bethany's two front teeth are missing, so she can't eat it very well. Joel used to eat everything; now he throws anything he doesn't want on the floor, and once the meal is over, if I don't sweep up quickly, he'll be down there nibbling at the crumbs!

Thinking of good food to eat sometimes drives me to distraction! Bernie and I like lots of salads and fresh fruit and simple stuff like that, but I haven't the time to make something different for each person. Nutrition is so complicated now! Gone are the days when you ate what you could get, and were glad of it. Today we know about cholesterol, vitamins and calories. We hear how this and that shouldn't be eaten together. You can be macrobiotic, wholefood, vegan, dairy-vegetarian, raw, gourmet, carnivorous or just plain junky. It's a minefield, and each diet seems to have a different map of where the mines are hidden!

Occasionally I will get adventurous and make a new dish. I'll indulge myself and spend lots of time in the kitchen creating a gourmet something-or-other. It's usually more 'other' than 'something', but at least it makes a change from spaghetti and pizza! (Where would we mothers be without the Italians?)

Proudly I place the latest concoction on the table, garnished delightfully with little hearts and flowers cut from carrots and cucumber, and wait for the response.

'That looks nice, darling.' Bernie is always grateful for his food, and will eat anything, no matter how disastrous the experiment. 'Bethany, it's your turn to say grace, please.'

'I don't want to.' She looks at the food — she's a truthful child, and she feels she can't truthfully say 'thank you' for something which looks as disgusting as that. She's sure that there must be a mushroom in it somewhere. Bernie says the grace.

Nathan stares at the food as if it is going to eat him. He doesn't say anything — he doesn't have to — his face says it all. 'Come on,' I say, 'have a little bit. I'll put it right over here so it doesn't touch the potatoes.' I put a spoonful on his plate, inches from any other food. Nathan's world suddenly falls apart.

'Aaarrrghh! I'm not eating anything now! You've spoilt everything! It will all be horrid!' He bursts into tears.

I offer some to Joel. He uses the spoon as a catapult to target the pale green carpet that the previous, child-less owner of our house had considerately fitted in our dining room.

Well, I'm going to enjoy it, anyway. I ignore the children. If they get hungry enough they'll eat, as my father used to say. It's not bad; in fact, it's really tasty.

Afterwards I clear up. Bethany has eaten everything on her plate. Bernie made Nathan taste the food by bribing him with a story. He virtually forced a tiny spoonful into his mouth. 'Mmmm,' said Nathan, 'that's nice, Mummy! Can I have some more?' Joel is down on the carpet mass-aging his ammunition into the pale fibres. The area around his place doesn't really look pale green any more, except where a pea had an accident. Bernie fin-ished up every last scrap in the dish.

God is a Father who wants to give the best things to His children. We sit at His table, where He has provided the perfectly-combined diet for each one of us. With more time and patience than most mothers have, He has catered for our individual, spiritual and nutritional needs, as well as our tastes. And as each course is served, what does He hear?

'Ugghhh! I don't like the look of that!'

'I'm not going to eat this stuff! Look! It's messed up all the other food on my plate!'

'I think I'll give mine to someone else.'

'I don't think I'm hungry any more.'

'I think I'll pop this in the bin when no one is looking!'

But there are those, who, even though they may feel a little apprehensive at the sight of an unexplored dish, trust in God's divine catering capabilities, and taste what He has offered them. They savour the delights of a gourmet treat, the perfect blending of flavours and ingredients, and their bodies feel strengthened and revitalized as they leave the table, taking something away to share with anyone they find who is hungry.

Dear Father, help me to trust in Your creative, loving wisdom. I know that You want to serve me only the best things You can offer to keep me healthy, happy and delightfully satisfied. Thank You for spreading such a wonderful banquet before me. Amen

How do you respond to the things which God is serving up to you in your life?

Think of a time when you turned your nose up at something God put on your plate, only to find out later that it was the perfect treat for you.

Let your children help to choose the menu for dinner today, and let them help to prepare the food, too. Even small children can chop soft fruits with a blunt knife to make fruit salad.

Crumpled treasures

The Christmas tree has come down from the attic. We have an 'environmentally friendly' tree, a pretty good plastic imitation that doesn't drop needles for our inquisitive baby to eat! It stands, bare and skeletal, at the end of the living room, shivering in the slight breeze from the window. We're waiting for the children to come home from school and help with the decorations. I open the boxes of tinsel, white silk angels, silver stars, doves, and the tiniest little boxes wrapped in iridescent paper with silver bows. A white-and-silver angel lies in a special box, waiting to be fixed on the top of the tree. Strings of little white hearts and beads are wrapped around old Christmas cards, along with silver stars. Another box is full of sparkly snowflakes. The twinkly white Christmas lights lie tangled in an old biscuit tin. Somewhere else there are four different sets of Nativity figures: a miniature set of simple wooden shapes, a set carved in olive wood from Bethlehem, an embroidered Nativity that I made before we had the children, and a set of salt-dough figures that I made as a child.

But there is also another box. This box has little card shapes, smothered with finger paint and glitter. An angel with a ping-pong-ball head and wonky wings; a lantern made from a cardboard tube; a little fat snowman covered in cotton balls with black paper buttons. A bell made from a plastic cup covered in silver foil. These are the real treasures, put together by tiny, chubby fingers, all covered in glue and paint. It doesn't matter that they are bent and misshapen, or that they don't co-ordinate with the rest of the decorations; they are special because my children made them for me. Their love transforms the paper and glitter into satin and diamonds.

Yesterday Bernie and I gave a seminar together. We were both still recovering from a vicious flu virus that left us with coughs and colds and little energy. It was an important seminar, helping to conclude and sum up a whole weekend of sharing and learning.

Today I have that 'morning-after' feeling, the time of analysis and retrospect, wondering how I could have done better, regretting a misplaced word, or a clumsy explanation that didn't seem to be clear. I feel bad, because as we were finishing the seminar I realized that we had been videoed, and I had coughed and spluttered my way through the whole session. I feel as if I ruined the special atmosphere of the weekend.

'Dear Father, I'm sorry, I really messed up. I wanted to do my best for Your glory, and I tried so hard to make it perfect, and we had bathed the whole project in prayer. I'm just not much of a speaker sometimes . . . .'

I pick up the angel Bethany made in kindergarten. The head is coming loose: I'll have to stick it back on.

'Karen, it's all right. You did the best you could, and you did it because you love Me. You are My child, and whatever you do for Me is beautiful because it's a gift of love. Just as you treasure this little broken angel, I treasure whatever is done for Me in love.'

Thank You, Father, for letting me glimpse the delight You have in even my clumsiest gifts to You. Amen.

Think about the things you treasure, and consider why they are so special to you.

What gift would you like to give to Jesus today? Don't worry that it's not perfect, give it anyway, He'll love it!

Help your children to make some simple gifts such as biscuits, Bible bookmarks, bunches of flowers, etc, to share with other people, then deliver the surprises and watch the delight in their faces!

My Mum — for ever

My Mum is definitely my best female friend. She's always there, she always listens and always cares and understands. She knows when to speak, and when I just need to spout forth for a while to get something off my chest, without any need for a response. She is always finding ways to bring me little bits of happiness, and I try to find special ways to show her my appreciation, but it's hard to find something in this world that will let her know just how wonderful I think she is. When we get to heaven I hope I shall find the perfect words or gift, but then, maybe just being together in heaven will be all the gift she'll ever want. After all, the greatest hope I have for my own children is being able to share eternity together.

She called the other day and we chatted about this and that.

'Mum,' I said, 'you know what Bethany just said to me . . . ? I can't believe it!'

'Yes, I know, you were just the same!'

'And Nathan, well he . . . !'

'I remember the trouble your Dad and I had when you went through that phase . . . .'

'Joel is teething again, and he keeps vomiting on me.'

'Oh, I'm so glad you two have grown up now, and all that is behind me!'

There's something, quite a lot of things really, about being a mum, that help you to appreciate your own mother more than ever! It's rather humbling to think of all the nappies she had to change, puddles she had to mop, clothes she washed, and meals she cooked. There are all those nights she walked the floor with us, the hours of concerned prayers when we were teenagers, the frustration of coping with our stubborn wills . . . . The list is endless. Who can count all the things a mother does for a child in a day, let alone a lifetime?

She taught me to read and enjoy good books. She showed me how much fun it was to make things with my own hands, and share them with others to bring delight and beauty to their lives. She encouraged me to write; helped me to discover a fulfilling career as an occupational therapist; and together we used our creativity to think up an unusual quiz for a church social, or a fun theme for a party. Years of helping her in the kitchen as we prepared for countless guests, or baked for church banquets, was a great way to learn about hospitality, and bulk-catering, vital to my ministry as a pastor's wife.

It's her birthday soon, and I always want to try to give her something that will express a little of my deep gratitude and love. She doesn't want me to spend a lot of money on her, I know, so I usually try to make something special. A cross-stitch picture of bears hugging, because she collects teddies. A hand-painted T-shirt. A wreath of dried flowers. A book of hand-written poetry. Once we sent her a little book of photos, showing a day in the life of the Holfords, together with little stories about what we get up to, as we don't see her very often. This year I'm thinking of making a salt-dough garland of fruits and flowers, painting it with delicate colours, and hanging it with ribbons . . . .

My grandma, my Mum's Mum, is still alive, and a precious part of the family. She 'came to the Lord' years ago, and nurtured her family through the difficult war years. She went to live with her children in Wales when they were evacuated from the soon-to-be-blitzed city of

Coventry. Grandpa, an air-raid warden, stayed behind and was one of the people who had to sift through the wreckage of the nights, uncovering the untold horrors beneath the brick-and-sandstone rubble and the twisted lead of Cathedral windows. I thank God for my grandparents, who brought up both my parents in Christian homes, and passed their heritage of faith down through to us.

It's all the years that went before us that help to make us what we are now. Our childhood experiences play a major part in creating the kinds of parents we become. Bits of faith, happy traditions, love and sharing are passed down from generation to generation. Unfortunately, some families also pass on deep, tragic sadnesses and cruel secrets, broken hearts and miserable habits. A difficult past may need years of prayers, counselling, and unconditional love to help heal its wounded memories. And, if we don't have parents, there is usually some positive figure in our life who has loved and nurtured us, and helped us adventure towards our potential, and drawn us closer to God.

Dear Father, thank You for a wonderful mother and grandmother who have cared for me in so many ways. Now, as I mother, I can truly appreciate their love and sacrifice for me. Thank You that no matter what our earthly parents are like, You are an ever-loving Parent who always wants the best for us. Help me to think up lovely ways to show my appreciation to You, and to my mother. Amen.

Write a letter to your mother, or someone else who nurtured you and helped you to discover your potential. Thank them for the positive influence they have had in your life. Write about your special memories.

Plan a surprise for a parent, grandparent, or other close and supportive relative or friend. Involve the whole family in the fun: making food; creating a home-made, personalized card; picking and arranging flowers, etc.

As a family, talk about heaven, and what it will be like to be there all together. Imagine what your mansion would be like. Whom would you like to meet and talk to? What would be the most exciting thing you'd like to do there? What would you say to Jesus?

Juggling balls

Something about me and balls is not compatible. The mere suggestion of a ball game can double my stress level. I can lose a game of tennis before I can manage to serve a ball over the net. At school I always tried to run as far away from the ball as possible; fielding in distant, obscure corners; and attempting to protect the goal areas, without ever having to come into contact with the offending object! As a child I was short-sighted for years without realizing it, and, by the time I had my first pair of glasses, years of ball-game humiliation had made a lasting impression on my memory.

So it was with some relief that I watched Joel kicking a ball in the garden, the day after he began to walk! Almost from birth he had had a fascination with balls. Someone had made him a Victorian patchwork ball as a baby gift, and he would hold it and cuddle it for hours. Then, as he grew older, he would throw it, as babies do, laughing, onto the floor, over and over again.

Joel would yell with delight at the sight of an orange, apple, or grapefruit, because it looked just like a ball too, and if you gave him one to hold, he would use it as a ball, or try to eat the skin.

Yesterday we went to a family sports' morning. Once again I found myself studiously trying to avoid contact with anything remotely spherical. I tried badminton, but I wasn't much good at that either, because I always expect the shuttlecock to bounce, and, for some strange reason, it never does!

Bernie and the children were happily batting balls over the nets in short tennis, and playing basket ball. Joel slept most of the time, but towards the end he woke and thought he was in wonderland because there were balls everywhere! The balls were all of the spongy type, and nice and squishy for him to hold. He ran along the edge of the courts, squealing with delight and collecting any ball that came his way. An out-of-control toddler is a liability where people are playing sport, so I gathered him up in my arms, together with his ball collection, which we had to redistribute among several ball-less tennis games. Unable to pick up balls himself, he now yelled at the other children, and pointed to every ball he could see. He yelled and yelled until someone picked the ball up and gave it to him. But he was running out of places to put the balls. He had one in each pocket, one in each hand, and one cuddled to his chest. Five was the most he could handle; after that, he always had to drop at least one ball in order to grab another.

I put him down for a few minutes, and watched him trying to gather balls, but always losing some as he reached out for more. He was like a little, clumsy juggler, struggling there, with balls going all over the place.

'I think you've got yourself another story for your book!' My friend smiled at Joel. 'Don't you ever feel like that! When will we ever learn that we can only hold so many balls at once? After that, every time we pick up one new responsibility, we have to drop some of the others, till we end up like Joel, clumsily juggling, and not doing anything very well!' She said this with feeling. We both knew — we'd been there, trying to be a mother, a housewife, cook, pastor's wife, church social organizer, children's department organizer, writer, interior designer, seamstress . . . . The list seemed endless. Some attractive 'balls' had bounced our way, and we'd tried to catch them for a while, but always something else had suffered. This year we had both decided we needed fewer 'balls', but this was only January and already all kinds of balls were bouncing around our feet, just waiting to be picked up. It was hard to know which ones to choose.

It was time to pack up, and Joel was very helpful as he picked the balls up one at a time, and dropped them slowly into their box.

Dear Father, there are so many busy 'balls' bouncing around in my life. Help me to concentrate on Your priorities for my life, so that I am not rushing around trying to gather them all. Help me to choose the most important 'balls' of sitting at Your feet, and listening to Your words, so that You can help me to choose the best 'balls' for my life. Amen.

What are the greatest priorities in your life?

List all the 'balls' that you are trying to hold at the moment. Prayerfully consider your list, and see if there are any that need to be dropped for a while because they make it harder for you to hold the most important 'balls': your relationship with God, and your relationship with your family.

Spend some time today having a special moment with God, a special moment with your spouse, and a special moment with each of your children.

Red stripes, pink flowers and orange polka dots

Before I had any children of my own, I would look at other people's children. Some always seemed to look immaculate. The little girls would have spotless dresses, all ruffles and frills; lace-edged socks, and co-ordinated hair accessories. The little boys even managed to look adorable in designer sweaters, Osh Gosh jeans and Kicker boots. Their faces were always clean and shiny, and their hair neat and well cut. Other children were noticed for some of the opposite reasons! Maybe a little girl would be wearing a red stripy sweater, a pink flowery skirt, and orange polka-dot socks! Or maybe there would be a sticky patch in her hair, or she had a very runny nose. Another boy might be wearing jeans with holes in the knees, and mud on his T-shirt, or bits of breakfast encrusted down his front. And I expect there were lots of children in between the two extremes that were never really noticed.

In those idealistic days before the reality of motherhood hit me (somewhere between the kitchen and the laundry basket!) I imagined my children would always fit into the first group. I was determined that they would always look perfect and clean and co-ordinated. For quite a while I managed to retain those high ideals! Bethany was given lots of cute little dresses and outfits; she wasn't a messy baby and we did quite well for a few months. Then we went to a wedding, a long way from home. It was raining. Bethany fell in a muddy puddle, head first, frills and smocking, lacy tights and white shoes. We fished her out, washed her in the ladies' toilets, and she spent the day in pyjamas, because that's all we had with us.

Bethany soon learned to dress herself, and she had strong opinions about clothes. So did I. I liked the thoroughly co-ordinated look, and pretty dresses; Bethany was into bright and cheerful — the more colours the merrier — and dresses were OK for church and special times, but leggings were her favourite things for everyday. I had to struggle with the dilemma of whether to let her choose her own clothes for the day, and then cope with my embarrassment, or choose her outfits for her, and cope with a miserable child. It was so frustrating to be going somewhere special, put her in an outfit that looked gorgeous, and have her in tears because it wasn't bright pink.

So far the boys haven't really minded too much what they wear; it's more a problem of what will *stick* to what they wear. Mud, paint, marker pens, oatmeal, ketchup, grass-stains, and an odd assortment of indefinable substances all seem to creep up on their clothes, and then hurl themselves with a great splat across their fresh T-shirts and jogging suits!

Once, when all of us had streaming colds, we were at church for a whole day, and I seemed to go from one runny nose to another. Joel sneezed when I was working on Nathan, and by the time I got to him, he was happily licking at something slimy dripping off his upper lip, in front of most of the church members! On close inspection the skin on his cheeks looked as if it had been crackle-glazed where he'd wiped his hands across his nose, and layer after layer had dried on to his skin! I was fairly fastidious with one child, moderately tidy with two, but with three — well, my standards have taken quite a tumble! If a little dampness leaks from Joel's nappy — I tend to let it air dry where it is, rather than face the hassle of changing him! There are days when

Nathan's hair never sees a brush, when (horror of horrors!) the children even go to bed without cleaning their teeth!

It's not that I don't care. I love to dress them all up and have them look smart and pretty, but a few years of mothering have taught me that looks don't matter so much. It's great to go for a romp in the woods and watch them climb up their favourite tree — a storm victim, it leans at a sixty degree angle against a sturdy oak, half of its roots still in the ground, keeping it alive. Its slope makes it an easy climb. We walk, run, crawl under bushes, climb, pick berries, gather sticks and stones and have a picnic. We sit in a flower-strewn glade in the warm-gold light of late afternoon. Our hair is tumbled, and sprigged with the odd dried leaf. Our hands are berry-stained, and Nathan's T-shirt is measled with wild strawberry juice. Moss has greened their shorts where they sat astride their climbing tree. Bethany has a grazed knee, the blood drying against her skin. But they glow with life and happiness, and all the things they have discovered down the familiar, ancient pathways.

Some things are more important than looks. In fact, when you think about it most things are. And it's more important to let children grow and discover, dig up the worms, mess with the paint, get biscuit mix all over their faces, and into their hair, pick the berries, and feel the cool moss against their summer-hot legs. I could mop and nag and change their clothes, and be forever wiping their faces, and pressing their ruffles, but that's no fun for any of us! It's what's inside that counts — little feelings that bruise easily, an emerging self-concept, a developing personal taste, a sense of freedom to explore, the permission to enjoy a messy moment, a sense of being loved no matter what they look like or get into.

I'm not perfect — occasionally the old standards will rise up in my mind, and I nag, or even yell, when confronted with a mess. I think of how long it will take to get the stain out again, or how much money something will cost to replace, instead of considering the tender feelings of little children who were only having fun, or were so engrossed in something, just for a little while, that they did not notice the grape juice at their elbow, or the mud on the pavement. I still have a lot to learn. But I have learned that there is more to do in life than tidy up the children. Bernie once bought me a cross-stitched plaque for my kitchen which says 'A clean house is a sign of a misspent life!' I guess you could say the same about clean kids!

What is going to matter in eternity? No one will care that the children were always immaculate and neatly pressed, that their noses were always wiped, and their faces gleamed like a soap advert, or that their colours always matched. What will matter are all the things that were built up inside the child; trust, love, and obedience; a sense of self-worth that says their feelings are more important than their clothes; and a strong character, encouraged by God-loving parents.

Tonight, as I peeled off my old sweat-suit, caked in mud, spit-ups, yoghurt, runny noses and biscuit dough, and dropped it into the laundry, and as I looked at my face, shadowed through lack of sleep, my hair twisted in knots by Joel's baby fingers while he drifted off to sleep in my arms; and as I noticed the wrinkles in my still saggy tummy, I thanked God that He sees through all the mess on the outside, and only looks into my heart!

Dear Father, thank You that You look at the bits of me that really matter — the bits I can take into eternity. Show me that true beauty is made in my heart, and the hearts of my children, and help me to spend more time nurturing beauty that will last forever, and less time worrying about transient appearances. Thank You, Amen.

List some of the beautiful things you would like to build into your children's characters. Make a list for each child, if you like.

Focusing on the things you have written in your lists, write out practical ways you can help to build forever-beauty into your children's characters.

Also, prayerfully ask how God can help you be more beautiful where it really counts.

Write a 'to do' list for today. Number the items on the list in order of importance. Then have a look at the list and see which things will really matter in a hundred years' time! Renumber the list if necessary! Pray about your list. Ask God to help you do the things that are truly most important. And ask Him to help you do the things that you need to do, in order to help your home run smoothly in the here and now.

How many times . . . ?

Bethany and Nathan have just piled themselves, and all their supplies for a day at school, into the car. Joel and I are left surveying the wreckage on the breakfast table, but I can't face it now. So we go into the lounge, and I sit, just soaking in the tranquillity of the moment, after a hectic couple of hours of morning-mania. Joel is having a feed; soon he will drop off to sleep, and I will have some time completely on my own. I plump up a pillow next to me, and find Bethany's reading book lurking underneath. She should have taken it this morning. How many times do I have to tell her to pack it in her backpack each evening, so it's all ready for the next day?

Come to think of it, I often wonder how many times I shall have to say something to the children until it becomes a habit, and second nature, and I can rest my frustrated voice. They have been going to school for months now. And yet, every morning, even though the routine is always the same, we still have to remind them to go downstairs and have a drink; come back up and get washed; get dressed; tuck in shirts/do up ties/pull up zippers/brush hair; go back downstairs; eat breakfast; have worship; clean teeth; collect lunch boxes; put shoes on; put jackets on; kiss Mummy good-bye; (sigh a big sigh of relief).

I don't know who is most relieved when they are in the car, and off at last. It's not that I want to see them go, but I don't want them to be late, or forget something important. I don't like to hear my voice nagging away each morning — but, if I don't keep on reminding them, Bethany will find a book and lose herself in C. S. Lewis's *Narnia*, or wander over the prairie with Laura Ingalls. Nathan will build something amazing out of Lego, usually a helicopter, or a space rocket. Wonderful childhood experiences, but not compatible with making it to school for the 8.55am whistle.

How many times do I have to tell them what to do each morning before they will be able to do everything on their own? Or is the list of requirements just more than a young child can handle in one go? Am I expecting too much of them? How can I get them through the routine without nagging? I keep meaning to make a check-list for each of them, reminding each one what to do, so it can nag for me, and I don't have to listen to my own tired voice over and over again. I'm sure the children would be grateful for the peace, too! Maybe they hear my voice say the same things so often that they have learned to tune out my droning! Or maybe it's much easier to be told what to do all the time. Maybe I should make a tape of my 'requests' and play it each morning to save my voice! I could even set the words to music, to make them more fun to listen to! Or I could compose a poem to remind them in rhyme!

Susannah Wesley, mother of twenty children, was once watched by a young man. Through the morning she was trying to teach one of her young sons to do something, something quite simple, like remembering to shut the door each time he wandered in and out of the room. Twenty times she calmly reminded him of what he needed to do, until it finally became a habit. The young man marvelled at her patience (so do I!) and said, 'Do you realize that you told that young lad the same thing twenty times this morning?'

'Yes,' she said, 'and if I had done it one time less, I would have failed him as a mother.'

How many times shall I have to tell my children what

to do each morning? I don't know. Seventy times seven sounds like a good number. I must find a way of helping to prompt them through the routine without damaging the children, or my relationship with them. But I will keep on telling them what to do until they don't need me to remind them any more. As a mother, what else can I do? . . .

After all, God still has to keep reminding me about many things: sometimes every day; sometimes twenty times a day. He doesn't nag. He reminds me gently, with love in His voice; He thinks up different ways to get the message across, to prevent me from 'tuning' Him out, or getting frustrated by His reminders. I want to remember, but sometimes it's all too much to cope with on my own, or I get distracted, or I forget what I'm doing, or I dawdle over something unimportant. But He keeps on, shaping me slowly, day by day, till one day He knows He will be able to stop, because I shall do it all on my own. Until then He reminds me seventy times seventy times seven. He knows if He does it fewer times He will have failed me as a Father.

Dear Father, thank You for being patient with me. Some good habits take a long time to grow. Help me to be patient with the children, knowing I am just a child in Your care, too. Amen.

List the habits you have that you would like to eliminate, and new ones you would like to acquire. Pray about each list, and work together with God on a strategy for growth.

Do you nag your children? What do you find yourself saying over and over again? Is there another way of teaching them, or another way of coping with the situation?

Pray for patience as you gently guide your children into good habits. Don't give up. Remember, it may take only one more reminder to establish a habit forever!

Why bother?

Sometimes I have a hard time wondering why I bother to go to church. Don't get me wrong. I love my church, and the week feels all wrong if I don't manage to make it there. But as a mum, and a pastor's wife, coping alone with three children in church can be such a draining experience, when what I most need is to be filled up by God. And that can be frustrating.

This week Bernie is preaching at a church we have never been to before.

I enter church in my usual dishevelled heap of 'happy bags' for the older two, and nappy bags for Joel. Everyone turns and stares at us. I gaze around desperately, trying to find a space with four chairs together. The back rows, labelled 'Reserved for parents with small children', are filled with teenagers and older people. Elsewhere, there are seats only in ones and twos. Someone, embarrassed, gets up and offers me one chair. I thank them, decline their generosity, and bravely set out for the front row.

Sometime during the second hymn, a child whispers, desperately, 'Mummy, I need to go, quickly!'

'OK,' I whisper back, 'can you manage on your own, because Joel's asleep in my arms and I don't want to disturb him?'

'Yes, Mum, I'll be all right.'

The hymn finishes, and the child still hasn't returned. The congregation hushes, and Bernie begins to preach. Suddenly there is a yell from the back of the church. A plaintive, but strong little voice: 'Mummy, Mummy, please will you wipe my bottom!' Pause. 'Mummy, Mummy, please will you wipe my bottom!' Pause. 'Mummy, Mummy, please will you wipe my bottom!' At home this little song continues until my footsteps are heard coming up the stairs.

I'm not sure what to do. There is nowhere to lay Joel, and if I move he will probably yell and yell, so I can't just drop him in someone's arms. The congregation is beginning to giggle, in a smothered sort of way. I turn and look at the back of the church, and watch as a dear, sweet person slips out. A few minutes later the child wanders back up the aisle, happy again and singing softly.

I prickle with awkwardness, and blush, and wonder what they are all thinking of me. Another child needs me to whisper a story from a children's Bible book. When the story is over I notice that the other child is lying on the floor, looking at a book — in the front aisle. I don't want to tell anyone off in church, but I feel the child really ought to sit next to me. I have to poke a leg with my toe to attract some attention, then the child says, a bit too loudly, 'Ouch, Mummy, why are you kicking me like that?' Joel wakes and burps noisily, then, even more loudly, fills a nappy. It is so obvious to the whole congregation that he's done something, that I feel obliged to change him. I leave the other two in the church, and make my way out, trapping the nappy bag in the heavy doors as I go, causing even more of a fuss.

I almost feel like staying outside, but I can't leave the other two unattended, so I have to go back in again. I know Bernie won't mind the disturbance, but I wonder what the other people will think about my 'unruly' little family!

The service is over, and it takes time to gather together all the children's bits and pieces. I linger a little over the sorting out so that I won't have to face so many people in the vestibule.

'Are these your children?' an older lady stops me on my way down the aisle. She looks warm and cosy and maternal. I feel safe with her.

'Yes. This is Bethany: she's 6; then Nathan, 4, and this is baby Joel.' Joel is all wriggly, and I can hardly hold all the bags as well. My arms ache from carrying him.

The lady smiles at me, and touches my arm. 'You are very rich,' she says, 'very rich indeed; and these,' she smiles at the children, 'are your greatest riches. You are so blessed to have three of them, and all so happy and healthy. It has been wonderful watching your loving family this morning. Thank you for coming.'

'You know,' she says, as she takes my bags, 'your family is one of the few treasures you can take into heaven with you. Treasure them now and you can treasure them forever!'

And then I know why I make the effort. I can't verbalize it exactly, but I know it's all worthwhile. In a few words, from a caring heart, God has filled me again for another week.

As we climb into the car, Bethany gives me a little note she wrote during the service. 'I love you, Mummy, and Jesus loves you too!' Her handwriting wobbles across the page, and there are flowers and hearts around the edge. Nathan laughs, and says, 'I liked that church! Can we come here again?' Joel's sunny smiles sparkle through every day, but they are no less precious because they are familiar. He grins as I fasten his car seat.

She was right, that lady. I am rich indeed.

Dear Father, thank You for the people You use to speak words of encouragement to me. Thank You that I am free to worship You with my children. Open my eyes and ears to find You speaking to me even when it can be hard to concentrate on the service. Thank You that I am rich indeed, and blessed with the love of little children. Amen.

What are your greatest treasures?

How does going to church make you feel?

Think of some things that your church could do to help make it easier for mothers and families to attend and to feel comfortable there. Talk to the pastor and see what simple changes could be made. For example — once a month, or so, baby-sitting can be arranged during the church service so mothers can listen without distractions. Sermons can be taped for mothers to listen to during the week. The main thoughts from the sermon can be printed in the bulletin, or placed on an overhead projector, so that mums don't miss them.

Start a journal, and each time you come home from church write down a thought that has lifted you up, that you want to hold on to through the week ahead.

Father and child reunion

I have always dreaded leaving my children anywhere without me. Even the thought of it gives me physical pain, as well as emotional stress. These little lives blended with mine for nine months, and even though the physical cord is cut, they are so much a part of me that when we aren't together I feel as if some part of me is missing, or numb, or even paralysed.

Sometimes it is wonderful to have a few moments on my own, to write, to run down a hill in the spring, to shop for presents and little treats with which to thrill their days. But there is always a sense of loss when they're not there, when there is silence in the house, and their jackets aren't hanging in the hall.

There'll be a day, all too soon, when they'll be gone. When all the mothering will be over, and all their rooms will be empty. So I want to make the most of every moment while they're here, to love them, and build them, and bind them to my heart, and to Jesus, forever.

I try not to cling to them too much. They need their space, their own friends, their own freedom. But it's kind of nice to hear one say, 'I wish I could stay at home with you all the time, Mummy.' Or, 'Mummy, when I have a baby, I want you and Daddy to come and live with me for three years, so I'll know what to do.'

It's hard to be apart for even a few hours, even when I know they are in safe hands. I know God's heart must ache a million more times than mine, to have to leave us here, where anything could happen to us, and often does. It must be so much harder to have to leave your children for several thousand years in such a dangerous place as earth. But we're not abandoned. We're not completely on our own. He is there to talk to every day. His Letters are available to read whenever we want to. But it must hurt Him every day that we're not together with Him in heaven. He must long to bring us home, to hold us, to share all that He's made and saved for us, and see us smile a smile that will never again see a tear of pain or loneliness.

He has left us, but not without a Comforter, Someone to care for us, and even to baby-sit us. He has left us, but not without the promise that one day He'll be back, and everything will be wonderful again. The ache I feel when I leave my child for a day is nothing to what He feels. I bet He can't wait to take us home! I'm sure He is just counting the days, itching to return, but waiting, because no child of His must be left behind, or left without the chance to become a part of His forever family. And one day enough will be enough, and He'll gather us all in His arms, and carry us into paradise, for eternity. It will be a Father and child reunion such as the universe has never seen before . . .

There's the chugging of a diesel engine, and the crunch of gravel in the drive. Joel yells out, and toddles down the hall to the front door. He pushes open the letter-box flap and peers outside, saying, 'Dada! Dada!' Nathan shouts, 'Daddy's home!' and rummages through his school bag to find the picture he made. It's bright and colourful, and Nathan told me it was he and Daddy flying our stunt kite over the hill. Bethany carefully puts her book down so that she doesn't lose her place, and wanders dreamily down the stairs. There is always a slight pause after Bernie parks the car in the garage. He has to fill out his mileage report for the day. The children wait expectantly, while I juggle the food in and out of the microwave for the third time.

Daddy says, 'Hello there!' to Joel, who is still looking out of the letter-box, then turns his key in the lock. 'Daddy! Daddy!' 'Daddy! Daddy!' The children throw themselves into his arms; drag him into the living room; sit him down and bounce on him. They all talk at once, telling him the stories of the day, tickling his feet, romping with him as he pretends to be a great hungry lion who tries to eat little children for supper, but the lion is always hungry, because the children always get away!

Daddy's home. We are together again. We are all safe and happy. And everything is wonderful. It's our father and child reunion. It's our little taste of a heavenly homecoming, here and now, just to remind us how much He wants to be with us, forever . . .

Dear Father, thank You for partings here, that make me long for a heaven without them. Thank You for happy homecomings that make me long for the final, forever homecoming. Thank You for showing us how much You long to be with us, and help me to be ready, waiting at the door when the time comes. I love You, Father, Amen.

Describe how you feel about being reunited with your Father God, forever.

What can you do to make your home a place where everyone can feel welcome?

This is the last chapter in the book. It's hard for me to say 'good bye' to the manuscript! How has reading this book affected the way you see God, and how has it affected the way you see your role in your own family?

Texts to encourage mothers, and others!

These texts could be the basis of your own personal promise box, or part of a spiritual journal; or the texts could be copied and shared with other mothers who need encouragement. This list is not exhaustive, so feel free to add other texts that have encouraged you.

'"The Lord does not look at the things man looks at. Man looks at the outward appearance, but the Lord looks at the heart."' 1 Samuel 16:7.

'For he will command his angels concerning you to guard you in all your ways; they will lift you up in their hands, so that you will not strike your foot against a stone.' Psalm 91:11.

'Come, let us bow down in worship, let us kneel before the Lord our Maker; for he is our God and we are the people of his pasture, the flock under his care.' Psalm 95:6.

'But from everlasting to everlasting the Lord's love is with those who fear him.' Psalm 103:17.

'He who watches over you will not slumber; indeed, he who watches over Israel will neither slumber nor sleep.' Psalm 121:3, 4.

'Sons are a heritage from the Lord, children a reward from him.' Psalm 127:3.

'For you created my inmost being; you knit me together in my mother's womb . . . . My frame was not hidden from you when I was made in the secret place.' Psalm 139:13, 15.

'I praise you because I am fearfully and wonderfully made; your works are wonderful, I know that full well.' Psalm 139:14.

'Train a child in the way he should go, and when he is old he will not turn from it.' Proverbs 22:6.

'Her children arise and call her blessed.' Proverbs 31:28.

'There is a time for everything, and a season for every activity under heaven: a time to be born and a time to die . . . .' Ecclesiastes 3:1, 2.

'He gathers the lambs in his arms and carries them close to his heart.' Isaiah 40:11.

'He gently leads those that have young.' Isaiah 40:11.

' "So do not fear, for I am with you; do not be dismayed, for I am your God. I will strengthen you and help you; I will uphold you with my righteous right hand." ' Isaiah 41:10.

'After the suffering of his soul, he will see the light of life and be satisfied; by knowledge of him my righteous servant will justify many, and he will bear their iniquities.' Isaiah 53:11 (using footnotes).

'For you will nurse and be satisfied at her comforting breasts; you will drink deeply and delight in her overflowing abundance.' Isaiah 66:11.

' "As a mother comforts her child, so will I comfort you." ' Isaiah 66:13.

'You will seek me and find me when you seek me with all your heart.' Jeremiah 29:13.

' "Therefore do not worry about tomorrow, for tomorrow will worry about itself. Each day has enough trouble of its own." ' Matthew 6:34.

' "Ask and it will be given to you . . . . For everyone who asks receives . . . ." ' Matthew 7:7, 8.

' "Which of you, if his son asks for bread, will give him a stone? Or if he asks for a fish, will give him a snake? If you, then, though you are evil, know how to give good gifts to your children, how much more will your Father in heaven give good gifts to those who ask him!" ' Matthew 7:9-11.

'At that time Jesus said, "I praise you, Father, Lord of heaven and earth, because you have hidden these things from the wise and learned, and revealed them to little children." ' Matthew 11:25.

' "Are not two sparrows sold for a penny? Yet not one of them will fall to the ground apart from the will of your Father. And even the very hairs on your head are all numbered. So don't be afraid; you are worth more than many sparrows." ' Matthew 10:29-31.

' "Come to me, all you who are weary and burdened, and I will give you rest. Take my yoke upon you and learn from me, for I am gentle and humble in heart, and you will find rest for your souls." ' Matthew 11:28, 29.

' "See that you do not look down on one of these little ones. For I tell you that their angels in heaven always see the face of my Father in heaven." ' Matthew 18:10.

' " 'I tell you the truth, whatever you did for one of the least of these brothers of mine, you did for me.' " ' Matthew 25:40.

' "Go home to your friends, and tell them how much the Lord has done for you, and how he has had mercy on you." ' Mark 5:19, RSV.

' "She did what she could. . . . " ' Mark 14:8.

'When Elizabeth heard Mary's greeting, the baby leaped in her womb, and Elizabeth was filled with the Holy Spirit.' Luke 1:41.

' "Martha, Martha," the Lord answered, "you are worried and upset about many things, but only one thing is needed. Mary has chosen what is better, and it will not be taken away from her." ' Luke 10:41, 42.

' "For the Son of Man came to seek and to save what was lost." ' Luke 19:10.

' "For God so loved the world that he gave his one and only Son, that whoever believes in him shall not perish but have eternal life." ' John 3:16.

' "And if I go and prepare a place for you, I will come back and take you to be with me that you also may be where I am." ' John 14:3.

'You see, at just the right time, when we were still powerless, Christ died for the ungodly. Very rarely will anyone die for a righteous man, though for a good man someone might possibly dare to die. But God demonstrates his own love for us in this: While we were still sinners, Christ died for us.' Romans 5:6-8.

'And we know that in all things God works for the good of those who love him.' Romans 8:28.

'For I am convinced that neither death nor life, neither angels or demons, neither the present nor the future, nor any powers, neither height nor depth, nor anything else in all creation, will be able to separate us from the love of God that is in Christ Jesus our Lord.' Romans 8:38, 39.

'Now we see but a poor reflection; then we shall see face to face. Now I know in part; then I shall know fully, even as I am fully known.' 1 Corinthians 13:12.

'And we, who with unveiled faces all reflect the Lord's glory, are being transformed into his likeness with ever-increasing glory, which comes from the Lord, who is the spirit.' 2 Corinthians 3:18.

'Therefore, if anyone is in Christ, he is a new creation; the old has gone, the new is come!' 2 Corinthians 5:17.

'"My grace is sufficient for you, for my power is made perfect in weakness."' 2 Corinthians 12:9.

'Do not be anxious about anything, but in everything, by prayer and petition, with thanksgiving, present your requests to God.' Philippians 4:6.

'Devote yourselves to prayer, being watchful and thankful.' Colossians 4:2.

'Pray continually.' 1 Thessalonians 5:17.

'May the God of peace . . . equip you with everything good for doing his will, and may he work in us what is pleasing to him, through Jesus Christ, to whom be glory for ever and ever. Amen.' Hebrews 13:20, 21.

'If any of you lacks wisdom, he should ask God, who gives generously to all without finding fault; and it will be given to him.' James 1:5.

'The prayer of a righteous (wo)man is powerful and effective.' James 5:16 (brackets supplied).

'Though you have not seen him, you love him; and even though you do not see him now, you believe in him and are filled with an inexpressible and glorious joy.' 1 Peter 1:8.

'This is love: not that we loved God, but that he loved us and sent his son as an atoning sacrifice for our sins.' 1 John 4:10.

' "He will wipe every tear from their eyes. There will be no more death or mourning or crying or pain, for the old order of things has passed away." ' Revelation 21:4.